ADVENTURES
IN SMALL BUSINESS

C. L. McManus

Artwork: Ahha Studios, Saint Louis, MO
© Copyright 2020 by C.L. McManus
All rights reserved, Published in the United States
ISBN #978-1-7358997-0-1 (paperback)

Some names and identifying details have been changed
and/or combined to protect their privacy.

To my husband Patrick
who supports my
hair-brained ideas,
for better or for worse…

To my customers who,
over time, brought out
the best in me

And to my employees who
joined me on this journey,
and helped me find my way.

Contents

One – That Looks Easy
"…it was anything but easy."

1

Two – Blissfully Unaware
"…I was as green as they came."

9

Three – What I was to Become
"…no weight was put on my own
genuine needs in starting a business."

19

Four – Cheats and Sneaks and Thieves
"Thievery was anticipated, but not in
as many forms as were to come."

29

Five – Obedience Class
"I would be on my best behavior (usually) when
it came to returns, complaints and requests."

39

Six - The Little Guy
"Everything from price increases to personal space
was different in the small store setting."

47

Seven - A Onesies and A Twosies
"Any woman can testify, a clean and inviting
public restroom is a rare and treasured thing."

59

Eight - What the FUTA
"I severely underestimated the vastness and depth of taxes and government paperwork."
67

Nine - The Retail Hamster Wheel
"…you aren't necessarily going to get to the legendary pot of gold."
77

INTERMISSION - 85

Ten – The Good, The Bad, and The Bosses
"…bosses came in a strangely wide variety."
89

Eleven – Sharing the Load
"…my job duties suddenly shifted from doing everything myself to delegating things to others."
97

Twelve - Puppies, Lattes & Sneaky Pete
"I naively expected a bunch of average Joes and Janes. More specifically, I expected GROWN UP Joes and Janes…"
105

Thirteen - Finding a New Perspective
"Thankfully, I began to change how I looked at things…"
113

Fourteen – That P.O.S.

"I needed a point-of-sale system, a.k.a., POS."

123

Fifteen – An Against You Kind of Day

"Technology and my bad view towards
it came to bite me…"

131

Sixteen – A Roller Coaster of Emotions

"All too clear are my prayers to get me out of it…"

139

Seventeen – The Lessons Learned

"The realization struck that although it's
turning a profit, it's not much of one."

149

Eighteen – Retail Roulette

"…I learned nothing is off-limits…"

159

Nineteen – Maybe Not

"I pulled myself back to reality, reminding myself of how
many times I said maybe and how many times it ended up
being 'maybe not.'"

169

Twenty – Goodbye Mr. Rogers Neighborhood

"…it's these same people that give me a sense of
routine and normality in a crazy world."

177

Introduction

Owning a small retail business is like opening the front door to your home and letting anyone walk in, browse, and use your bathroom. They can then decide to do one of three things: buy some of your stuff, steal some, or walk out with a simple "meh." Everyone shops, but few give much thought to the struggles of the small brick-and-mortar stores. I gave no thought regarding their concerns until owning one. There was very little fear as the thought process swam in my head, "Really, how hard can it be?" Well, remember that scene in Star Wars when young Luke Skywalker talks to Yoda and says, "I'm not afraid." Yoda replies, "Oh, you will be, you WILL be." My approach to opening my own small store was with the same confident but naïve attitude as Luke.

When considering the notion years ago, I spoke to a friend who owned a small business. Her words of advice were blunt, "If you want to end up divorced and ruining your life, by all means, open one up." Those words stopped me in my tracks for about 15 years, but the impulse struck again in my late 40's. Having worked most of my life for others, I decided to leave the safety of a cubicle and weekly pay to take my sideline interest in door-to-door cosmetics a step further. Opening a small store in a strip mall was an eye-opener.

These pages incorporate the seriousness of debt and risk, along with the unexpected experiences of working alongside the public. For the most part, the latter is

written with humor to convey my amazement as they filed in. Feeling like there was a social experiment around me, I often smiled and thought to myself, "really?" and "wow!" After struggling with low self-confidence for most of my life, observing the actions of others gave me a gift: I wasn't so inept after all, or so different either. More surprising were the kind words and actions from others. Though I own multiple t-shirts that say, "it's way too peopley outside," I ultimately came to appreciate the differences in us, and more importantly, the kindnesses.

Anyone who finds human behavior fascinating, this is for you. Anyone owning or considering owning a small brick-and-mortar store, I've got advice and some cringe-worthy material for you as well. I hope that you enjoy the sense of humor in both my personal and business stories while discovering a new appreciation for "the little guy."

In hindsight, I would have been financially secure by remaining in a traditional job with a lot less stress. There were nights my prayers included pleading with God to "make it go away." God said no, so my obligatory adventure continued. However, as Zig Ziglar said, "What you get by achieving your goals is not as important as what you become by achieving your goals." By far, I am stronger and more rounded for having experienced the challenge of small business ownership.

"I'm ready for my money tsunami now…"

Chapter 1
That Looks Easy

The question, "what were you thinking?" crosses my mind a lot. And when it comes to opening my own small retail store, I still scratch my head. Working with the public shouldn't have even been in my vocabulary. I'm not what you would call a people person; I'm a Trekkie, and all that implies. I've even been to a Star Trek convention. I feel safer in the shelter of few emotions and the company of the likes of Spock. Yet, I was to enter the realm of owning a small store in an arena of unpredictable mood swings as I worked not only with the public but predominantly with women shoppers.

Store ownership and the public arena taught me several things. One, the words "are you the owner?" raises the owner's heart rate alarmingly fast. Two, sharing a small bathroom with the public in a relatively small space gives new meaning to the words personal space. Lastly, owning a small business is like getting married. You're in it for the long haul, for better, for worse, for richer, for poorer. And like marriage, there's a learning curve. You learn it's best to keep your mouth shut more often than not.

This life-changing experience in retail came about through my ongoing search for the meaning of life. It had me moving from city to city often, moving furniture in every room of every house very often, and changing

1

jobs more than I should have. When changing jobs in my field didn't fill the void (nor did rearranging furniture), I changed gears with a "what the heck, why not" stance. I did a U-turn from a career in engineering and surveying to open a brick-and-mortar retail store, and began to work mostly with women. I would find women will tell you shockingly personal information in an incredibly short time. Men won't tell you, much of anything. My old world of a cubicle adorned with photos of my kids and dogs, and cut-outs of memes that only a handful of people found funny was a warm cocoon. Those memes were one of the few extensions of my personality; by and large, I kept to myself. Things were about to change.

After having sold beauty products as a side gig, I watched as others did it full-time in the shopping mall setting. Besides the obvious attraction of being your own boss, I naively thought to myself, "well, that looks easy, REALLY easy!" Although the notion of "that looks easy" fueled my decision-making, it was anything but easy.

For instance, the depth of problems was from seemingly another realm. An email popped into my store account from the credit card processor stating, "A network upgrade in January might affect your orbital integration." Uh, English, please! However, the real shock was transitioning from avoiding people in my work cubicle to surrounding myself with them in a store.

Spoiler alert, the small business owner does not, in the end, retire to a multi-million-dollar condo in Aspen.

However, I gained a fair bit of knowledge between should I open a store?" to "well shoot, maybe it's time to close my cute little store." What ended up being a nine-year adventure was a personal transformation. Like the grinch, my small heart grew three sizes because, in the end, I missed the people previously warded off with a wooden stake and garlic around my neck. I still miss them; never in a million years did I see that coming.

In writing stories for this book, I laughed quite a bit. Conveying the facts along with genuine humor became a joy. Laughter can make most any situation into something light, and honestly, it's in most every nook of every cranny. For example, I chuckled at an eye-opening comment from a ten-year-old that reminded me that everything is a matter of perspective. He noticed some retro items from the 1970s displayed in the store, on a shelf, for decoration. He excitedly and seriously shouted out to his mother, "Hey mom, they got stuff from the 1900s here!"

It still makes me smile when I think about what I so bluntly said to my "phone husband," the nickname a customer fittingly applied to himself. He had phoned and asked, "Are you open tomorrow?" He sounded amazingly like my husband, so on the assumption that he's merely asking if I was working the next day, I honestly replied, "I'll come in if I feel like it." Yikes! That answer bordered on rude and was beyond puzzling, so he asked again, "Are you open tomorrow?" to which I repeated myself with extra clarification, "Well, one of the other gals is working, and I'll come in if I'm up to it." This time he sounded downright ticked off and said, "are you OPEN tomorrow?!" to which I realized this most certainly isn't my husband and, what's more, probably thinks I'm crazy. Quickly apologizing with an explanation that I thought he was my husband, I heard a bit of a chuckle on the other end. The next day a guy walked in the store and came up to me and asked, "Are you the owner?" When I replied "yes," the man now with a grin on his face and considerably lighter-hearted than the day before said, "I'm your phone husband, and my wife thinks this is pretty funny."

There were plenty of women that bonded with me for a brief moment as we mused about shared problems, like the single and coarse hair we all seem to get on our chin when we turn 50. I mentioned that I tug on mine and play with it while watching TV, and my customer laughed and chimed in quickly with "Me too!"

Of course, there is an underlying seriousness to most of it, and it was difficult to find funny in taxes, but there was humor in that as well. There had to be, for sanity's sake.

Before the store, my roller coaster career spanned 15 places of employment, so it was only a matter of time before retail would be back on the menu. My work experience began re-shelving books at age 14 at the local library; that lasted two years. Next, I served time in the fast-food industry for six months, which was six months too long. I worked for about a month as a dental assistant, not my cup of tea, and two weeks at a collection agency, also not my cup of tea. After a few months in the deli department of a grocery store, I found that spearing skewers through the armpits of chickens in preparation for the spit, undesirable. Nonetheless, fast food and chicken prep did give me an appreciation for future jobs under far more pleasant conditions.

My work at a variety store, similar to a Walmart, lasted for three years. Though I was young, my experience at the store was a precursor to owning my own. I was a square peg in a square hole. My freaky straightening skills, bordering on OCD, were a joy as my job often called for me to straighten, and time passed quickly, almost too quickly. Cashier work at the register and just about every department in the store were included in my duties, as well as the toy department during the eighties Cabbage Patch doll craze. It was an early lesson in customer psychology. My powers to not only enter the stockroom but to snag a highly sought-after doll for an anxious mother was similar to a superpower. At least that's the way I felt as I handed over the coveted doll to a beaming mother.

And finally, drafting house plans at a local lumber yard overlapped several other jobs and college. I earned my bachelor's degree in civil engineering and land surveying and spent 25 years toggling between eight different companies in my field in four different states.

After deciding to revisit retail, I picked the owners' brains during visits with nine other stores similar to what I would be opening. There were many dire warnings, which I chose to ignore, mixed with a great deal of complaining, which I also ignored. Although those two red flags should have stopped me, they say you see what you want to see. I saw an opportunity to do things my way, and also thought that doing things my way would dictate the money earned. Wrong! Instead of asking myself, "how much did I make today?" instead, the question, "how much did I lose today?" presented itself. This adventure would be, however, unlike any previous job. There was a lot more to it than selling items and balancing books. I had the fortunate experience of a job that included "people watching."

Watching people is fun; watching families is fascinating. Three female family members walked in: a mother, daughter, and an aunt who was visiting from out of town. They spent upwards of an hour and had non-stop conversations. The aunt was eccentric, the daughter was at her wit's end, and the mother tried to keep everyone happy. While the aunt chose items willy-nilly like a squirrel gathering nuts, the daughter became increasingly impatient and rolled her eyes as she watched the stockpile grow on the checkout counter. Auntie paid no mind to price either, making me hyperventilate, in a good way. The mother, a modern-day June Cleaver, quietly appeased her guest while lovingly smiling at her daughter who looked to be "on the edge." It was genuinely entertaining to watch, and I've often said, "If only I could videotape this, it'd make a great sitcom." When they finally lined up to make their purchases, the daughter was exhausted, so I said under my breath, "there's some Tylenol in the back if you need some," to which she replied, "Do you have any straight Vodka?" Watching them interact made it clear; there was something to a store that family and friends wanted to hang out in. The big bucks weren't rolling in, but something worthy had been created.

My expectations in opening a store included control over decisions, personal time, and of course, cash flow. It could potentially be fun, and if good fortune were in the cards, I'd earn far more than in jobs past. Essentially, I was expecting just another job but with more control.

In reality, it was anything but just another job. There was more control in some respects, but I had no control over the seemingly endless flood of cash to those who would profit from my profit. On the plus side, there was a lot of unexpected humor and camaraderie that would slowly break my rigid exterior. I never thought I'd get attached to the connections with people; it wasn't in my nature, but by the end, I did. Thus, this book takes off at the fork in the road of expectations and reality...

"Sign this 40-page lease…unless, of course, you think you're out of your league"

Chapter 2
Blissfully Unaware

First things first, we needed a location. A strip mall a half an hour from home seemed to be up and coming. After lining up a meeting with the landlord, my husband and I nervously sat behind a large table in a very large boardroom. Intimidation lay in the air as the framed photographs of all the significant properties this guy owned screamed at me, "you're out of your league!" It was the first genuine feeling that things were about to change. His minion walked in and went over the basics while I tried to appear like this wasn't all brand new to me. After handing him my business plan and answering his questions, we waited for him to say something along the lines of, "you're not really what we're looking for." Surprisingly he gave me the paperwork to proceed.

A lawyer reviewed our 40-page lease, yes 40 pages, then advised us what to ask for, including as short of a lease as possible. The confidence my lawyer had in my little adventure was overwhelming. The landlord wanted us to sign a five-year lease; we asked for one but settled on three. This triggered a series of prayers with God involving various deals and pledges to give me a do-over to resume my former tedious but safe life. It was a real pity party. Then, between praying and crying, the grueling process of navigating the city, county, and state rules and regulations for various permits began. It can be summed up in one word, wow.

Regarding knowing what to expect with the lease or the improvements necessary to open my store, I was as green as they came. It wasn't until I spoke with another small business that I even heard of requesting money upfront to assist with carpet, paint, and other build-out expenses. They told me to negotiate for a fair amount of money for the "build-out cost" as a part of the lease signing. I nodded and smirked as though I had just heard some big secret; it wasn't. Most landlords wouldn't happily volunteer this tidbit, but most tenants aren't quite as naïve as I was either. Luckily, the information did find its way to me, as the extra money to prepare the space made all the difference. The only "glitch" was a three-year lease.

Weeks before the official first day of business, we opened a bank account to "deposit all that money." Delusion had set in. The bank employee handed me a zippered vinyl bank deposit bag, which looked incredibly small, so I very seriously and excitedly said, "You better give me two!" That second bag sat on the shelf for the next decade, collecting dust. Reality hit home soon afterward; there would be no money tsunami roaring my way.

Blissfully unaware of the events to come, we opened our small retail store on December 9th, 2011. What was to become our 2nd home for almost a decade measured 20' by 80'. The 1600 s.f. included a small office and bathroom leaving 1200 s.f. of retail space. It began as a stark room with a concrete floor and unpainted drywall but quickly transformed over a couple of months as we carpeted and painted it with warm earth tones.

We lined the walls with slat wall shelving, filling the rest of the space with glass displays and white wood cube units. Whatever part of your brain signaling danger must've been asleep that entire initial period because my internal autopilot pointed, signed things, and said, "yeppers!" all with this weird confidence and enthusiasm.

Ours was not a typical franchise, so we were left to our own devices to correctly organize and display our inventory. My husband played along and handcrafted the most significant piece in the store, a beautiful cash wrap to house the register and computer systems, bags, outside orders, and brochures. We were creative in piecing together preowned fixtures from other stores liquidating with new, pricier pieces on a frighteningly small shoestring budget. It was sobering to purchase items from another small store that had decided to call it quits. We bought a desk and décor at significantly discounted prices from this poor couple closing their business.

The couple stood amongst their vanishing dream in a now mostly empty location. They briefly touched on their difficulties, but I'm not sure I wanted to know. We were already in the game and needed to stay upbeat. I mentally distanced myself and thought, "They couldn't make it work, but we can."

Looking on with hopefulness, I gave my new carpet, paint, and intricate cash register system the once over. We filled the fixtures with tidy rows of products, primarily cosmetics, perfumes, skincare, and bath and body inventory. Straightening my back with my head held high, a slightly disillusioned voice said, "Wow, look at you! You're an entrepreneur!" Both excitement and nausea filled me. Was this the right thing to do? My knack for organization and an ever-present desire for change and adventure was real. On the flip side, I'd never managed anything except myself, and I'm not sure I did that all that well. My work experience had nothing to do with retail. Nevertheless, I moved forward with an "it'll all work out" boldness.

The days before the official opening were terrifying, especially the 24 hours prior. It's like being pulled up to the peak of a roller coaster while checking that the crossbar holding you secure is indeed tight, but fully expecting it to give way. Pondering why I put myself in such a vulnerable position, I wondered if maybe I did bite off more than I could chew this time. Luckily, a good friend arrived from out of town to support me. Woefully unprepared with the final setup, my emotions were mushrooming. She had to see it but never let on.

"Good friends don't let friends do stupid things…alone"
– author unknown.

Instead, she grabbed the reigns and assisted in arranging things, and didn't allow my anxiety to get the best of me. She stayed with me at the store until 3 am, and returned with me mere hours later for opening day. And when my budding comfort zone was challenged early on in those first couple of days with a young, blind customer, my friend offered her assistance and her arm, guiding her around my new store. I was very fortunate.

The business checkbook took a hit while decorating the space to make my customers feel at home. A high-quality sound system hooked to a stereo and big screen TV was a luxury but part of the overall plan. The plan was to create a general vibe of calm, including playing movies appropriate for my primarily female shoppers.

Appropriate became a word that, had I invested a little more thought, wouldn't have turned to bite me one January morning…

"The Goodbye Customer" was a very bad day, one month after opening on a slow, January morning. There was no one, and I mean no one, walking through the door for the first 90 minutes. I'm in the back office working on my computer while a movie plays on the stores' rather large flatscreen TV. While initially setting up the store, my desire to create something special was all about setting me apart from the big box stores. This included playing movies appealing to my mostly female shoppers. I hoped that it would make them feel relaxed and at home. That day I chose to play *The Goodbye Girl* with Richard Dreyfuss, a seemingly safe film to fit the image I was trying to create. A lesson was lurking around the corner. While pounding away at the computer, the familiar "ding" from the doorbell rigged to chime when opening the front door made me smile. I thought to myself, "Ah, finally, a customer." Bounding out to the front of the store, my eyes bolted first to the customer, and almost simultaneously to a stripper, in full stripper mode, dancing on my big screen in a G-string to, what else, stripper music. After a significant "this can't be happening" moment, I beelined it to the TV. While the strippers' double lattes were jiggling back and forth, a - year-olds shrinking voice came out of my mouth as I said, "Can you believe this? I thought this was a safe PG movie and never thought *The Goodbye Girl* would have a scene

14

like THIS!" At the same time, I'm wincing and recoiling, with a second set of eyeballs looking out the side of my head at this woman in her late 50's who is not buying this uncomfortable explanation. While attempting to prove to her as one would try to prove to their parents, "See, I am a good kid!" I pop out the video and march it straight to the trashcan, literally. She still hasn't said a WORD to reassure me. What kind of cruel karma would possess this woman to walk in during the 10-second window this scene would be playing? Damn you, Murphy's law! There's been nobody through the door all morning. Mumbling, "Is there anything I can help you with?" she replies, well, to be honest, I don't know what she replied with because the whole thing seriously disturbed me. Slinking to the back office to find a safe movie, I'm startled by the sound of the bell with her exiting through the front door. She left... pretty quick. Now convinced that she will tell everyone that my little store is quite a bit more than just cosmetics, I reach for the phone through my tunnel vision, phoning my sister for calming reassurance, who simply replied, "I guess *The Goodbye Girl* is really The Goodbye Customer."

My careless actions cost me a customer. Mistakes are expected; moving on is necessary. In the grand scheme, it wasn't that big of a deal and was, sort of, humorous. On the flip side, my daily exposure to the public gave me a window to observe things that aren't humorous or pretty. My upbringing was somewhat sheltered, my exposure to drugs was minimal, and it didn't take much to surprise me. When a young man trudged in my store, obviously high on something more than pot, I fell silent. He slowly walked the store's perimeter, not looking at me, or for that matter, anything. He simply put one foot in front of the other and stared straight ahead in an awful trance. It was clear he had no idea where he was, and it was sad to watch. Standing vigilant by my police emergency call button seemed pointless; I don't believe he was able to do anything other than breathe and trudge along. After completing his loop, he slowly walked back out and continued his painful journey.

"Whenever you feel like criticizing anyone, just remember that all the people in this world haven't had the advantages that you've had."
- F. Scott Fitzgerald

Bear in mind my store was in a very typical middle-class neighborhood. My now consistent exposure to the public arena made it clear how widespread drug addiction is. Another day (another year) a second guy staggered along the sidewalk in front of the nearby stores. He then collapsed in front of mine, seemingly from alcohol and a lot of it. He could pick up his head but not much more. Thinking to myself, "well, that doesn't look too good," I called the police to assist. By assist, I mean to have them completely take care of the matter, for which I remain forever grateful. A female officer quickly showed up and knelt by the man, and retrieved a water bottle from her car to hydrate his alcohol-drenched blood. The temps were in the nineties, and the sun was beating down, which only exasperated his condition. She showed an astonishing amount of compassion while waiting for an ambulance as I looked on from the safety of my bubble.

And then there was "Dolly," one of several actual customers who would look out for my safety. She was my most full of life and fun customer, though she took me a bit out of my comfort zone. She is as much an extrovert as I am an introvert. Picture a bubbly Dolly Parton with a sailors' mouth. Topsy turvy, I know. Dolly would routinely use the F word in conversation like the rest of us use the word the. Yet, despite her colorful language, she's a fun and good person. I found out just how good when she was alone in the store with me, and a questionable guy walked in; something didn't feel right. Guys rarely shopped at my store, and when they did, they certainly didn't linger. She purposely stayed in the store until he left, then she said, "I wasn't going to leave you alone." She held up her fists while she did a short dance, like a boxer, and finished by saying, "I was ready to fight him." She flashed that great smile of hers, and it was touching to know she cared enough to look out for me even if it meant putting herself in an uncertain situation.

My expectations of the store setup and operation was that of orderly precision, and nothing out of the ordinary.

In reality, there's a lot to know about operating a small store. I experienced curveballs with the public in addition to the day-to-day operations. My "looks easy" mindsight was a misstep; I truly was blissfully unaware.

"The Customer is always right, right??"

Chapter 3
What I was to Become

Owning a store drove home the difference between generosity and placing a small value on my products and livelihood. Reducing a price when a customer didn't want to pay the shelf price was clearly unwise. But in the early days of wanting to please everyone, I did follow the adage "the customer is always right." I often reduced prices and needed to reanalyze my entire initial attitude. And when handing out excessive freebies to charity, I thought in terms of simple kindness. But no weight was put on my own genuine needs in starting a business. Rarely holding my ground initially, I realized that Zig Ziglar was correct; it was important what I was to become by achieving my goals. As my needs came to light, I slowly began to change. I learned, with time, to draw boundaries. Unfortunately, this following story was not that day...

Honesty is all well and good, as long as you don't have to be too honest. This sage advice came from a customer in a roundabout way. After making an $80 purchase, a customer calls asking why there was an $80 credit to her account instead of an $80 debit. After some research, we discovered that one of my employees had inadvertently put the purchase through as a return. My customer understands and offers to reverse the charge; her scruples brought back my faith in humanity. That was all well and good until I explained that I'd be putting through a total of a $160 charge. Not only did the mistaken credit need reversing, but the original charge of $80 still had to go through. Like a deer caught in the headlights, the words, "whoa whoa whoa" ran through her head. Freak out mode begins as she realizes her honesty isn't sounding too good now. After noticing her reaction, and before this honesty thing got out of hand, I offered to reverse the credit, letting the original purchase go. She would essentially be given the $80 in product for free while cutting my losses with the thought that at least I'm not out the merchandise AND the $80. The moral of the story, most people like to be honest, but not too honest.

At the time, I felt confident that I did the right thing; recouping some loss without making waves was the safe path to take. I was all about not making waves, and it seemed like meeting halfway was the right thing to do. The problem was, I was all too eager to take losses, while those on the receiving end seemed far too eager to accept. In hindsight, backing down so quickly shouldn't have been as second nature as it was.

A levelheaded conversation mixed with a dab of sympathy for her position probably would've gone a long way in producing the entire $160. I appreciated her honesty in coming forward, but the fact remained that she owed the store $160, not $80. Had things become heated, backing down was always there and could've been pulled out of the hat. I could have offered a discount on her original purchase and recouped the majority of the loss while still providing an apology/thank you discount.

20

Unfortunately, as a new and inexperienced store owner, my willingness to sacrifice myself was all too quick.

It wasn't long into owning the business before it was clear there was an alarming trend and escalating rate in those who approached me for charitable donations. I've always been a giving person and have been in their shoes. I could never understand why any business wouldn't donate a little something, and wow, it was a personal attack when someone said no to me. I now understand. There were days that the first two to three people in the door were there only to ask me to donate to their upcoming fundraiser. And not a single paying customer had walked through the door yet that day!

In the first few years, donations of baskets filled with a considerable amount of product were lined up for pickup. Over the years, the baskets and their value shrunk in size, and finally, the question was asked of myself, "Why am I simply giving merchandise away with no reason for them to step foot in my store?" At this point, the recipients began receiving $25 gift cards to the store so they would have to come in, buy something, and create an awareness that my little store even existed.

It was a humbling realization that as much as I wanted to be a prosperous business owner/philanthropist, it just wasn't feasible at that point. Minimizing donations were necessary after realizing my business loan wasn't getting any smaller. I've been there, volunteered for not-for-profit organizations, and understood that they wouldn't exist without donors. Still, I've learned from my own small business that during those first years, you're doing nothing but trying to keep your head above water, and donating to charity, while admirable, isn't wise. There is no extra money at the start, period.

Another drain on the bottom line was product returns. They are normal and expected, but they hit a small business especially hard. I learned it's ok sometimes to say no if their request fell outside established guidelines. In the beginning, however, it was all about bending over backward and validating the mindset that the customer is always right. And quite honestly, it was just easier.

Loving like Jesus was presented in an odd way when a customer walked in, guilt-free, and said, "I need to return this mascara purchased a week ago; the wand broke." I'm thinking to myself, "A week ago, huh…that was discontinued and sold out over a year ago." Going on the motto of choosing your battles wisely overruled the decision to engage with the ease of proceeding with a relatively small return. As she turned to leave the store, it seemed ironic that the back of her t-shirt displayed the message, "Love Like Jesus." The whole scene struck me as humorous. After relaying the story to my husband later that day, he too chuckled as he chimed in with, "Love like Jesus but lie like Satan!"

These small but numerous moments were unexpected and funny, adding to the experience of owning a small business. Although most of the transactions were

22

uneventful, some sauntered in providing challenge, humor, and a stark realization of how animated and even feisty we all are.

While freebies, mistakes, and returns nickel and dimed the bottom line, they also added to the glaring realization of how self-employment would play out in the financial stress arena. Years before, my friend had clued me in with the blunt advice on business ownership, "If you want to end up divorced and ruining your life, by all means, open one up." I disregarded it as I've always had an "it'll be ok" attitude, an ironic approach to life since worrying is like breathing for me.

In the very beginning, I was ignorantly bliss. But blissful is not the description I'd give those first few years. Entrepreneur.com sums it up nicely by saying, "The problem is you don't know when or if the payoff will come. That means having to withstand long periods of uncertainty with no discernible progress while bleeding resources and making decisions based on ever-changing market conditions." We honestly didn't know when or even if the payoff would come.

A certain amount had to go through that register every month to pay the rent, which was considerable for small businesses. At $3000 a month for 1600 s.f. and roughly 40% earnings after product cost, theft, and coupons, the store had to sell $7500 every month JUST to pay the rent. Adding to that burden was the type of items selling, relatively low dollar items. We weren't selling computers or pricey handbags but rather makeup and lotions. We had to sell a heck of a lot of mascara and eye-liner to pay the rent.

Before we had the store, my husband had a boss whose father owned an ice cream shop. He didn't own it long because, as he put it, "You have to sell a sh*tload of ice cream cones just to pay the rent." We found out exactly where he was coming from and were in a similar situation.

We settled on a space in a strip mall after having looked at the much larger indoor malls. The shocking amount of $3000 a month for rent ended up being a bargain compared to the $4000-$8000 the indoor malls commanded for a small space.

I sat across from the leasing agent who represented a busy indoor mall, feeling slightly out of my league as she went on to explain. I could get into a spot, for around $4000 a month, if I were willing to sign a lease where they could move me, anytime they found fit, to anywhere they saw fit, within the mall. The bottom line, if another tenant wanted my space and was willing to pay the higher amount, my store would get the boot. Paying closer to $8000 a month for a permanent space was the only way to lock in a location. Waaaay too much risk, no thank you. However, it was a hefty dose of humility as I scampered out with my tail in-between my legs.

In addition to rent, the store had to pull in an extra and considerable amount to pay utilities, advertising, employees and have enough left over to restock the product. I found myself habitually walking to the register while mumbling, "please, please, please," to check the daily totals, then breaking out in a sweat if they weren't anywhere near where I wanted them and NEEDED them to be. It took five years before the comfort of the ebb and tide of sales set in and a vigil was no longer required. A high Wednesday would offset a low Monday; a high April would offset a disappointing March or May.

My stress level would leach into my home life, something no amount of study could prepare me for. With too much on my plate initially, I was a pressure cooker and classically internalized things until the hissing, rattling, and explosion finally occurred.

My husband worked the financial end and would ramp up my anxiety by saying things like, "OMG, do you realize how much we owe on the business credit card?" He magnified it by saying, "I don't think you realize..." It was a bit condescending and part of his routine, like brushing his teeth. Every time I heard it, my hackles stood on end, and on a good day, I would put a cork in it.

Not only did I realize it, but we were in a sink-or-swim situation for years. Either bite the bullet and stock the retail space properly or own a store with partially filled shelves only to die a slow death. With our investment in it, we almost had to bank on eventually making it and push through those first few terrifying years. He reluctantly agreed, nonetheless he continued for years with the "I don't think you realize…" statements while I pawed at the ground like a raging bull.

But, though tempting, we weren't going to throw in the towel even with the inevitable hissy fit that made its appearance from time to time. There were advantages; my disabled son could accompany me to work at a moments' notice. He had his own space, TV, toys, and lounger in my office. The hours weren't bad and were somewhat flexible with time off as needed for family and vacations. However, it was close to a decade before I would be close to "walking away" while hiring the whole thing out. That was my ultimate goal; it just took much longer than anticipated and a terrifying roller coaster ride along the way.

There was a store clerk who'd confess
Little knowledge of retail success
So sure she could run
And have lots of fun
A store but found out she was clueless

I expected to set the store in motion with relative ease and have it run pretty much on its own, like a well-oiled machine. I didn't anticipate how long it would take for this to happen. It would be close to a decade later when I would finally entertain the thought that maybe the store WOULD be self-sufficient. But, fate had other ideas.

26

The reality was an abyss of unexpected bills, problem-solving, and continually trying to do things just a little bit better. I was forever saying, "Now, what's that?!" Moreover, there was a new maturity in admitting that I had to make changes, and fast. Reaching the sweet spot of having the store run on its' own would be, slow at best.

"*You own a store, you can absorb
a little loss here and there…*"

Chapter 4
Cheats and Sneaks and Thieves

Thievery was anticipated, but not in as many forms as were to come. It's personal for a small business, and therein lies the REAL problem. I took everything personally in the beginning and couldn't let it go with constructive problem-solving. So instead, I framed quotes about stealing from a small business and positioned them around the store like a mom yelling at her kids. It was ridiculous, but I hoped that if enough passive-aggressive notes got their attention, people would think, "whoa, better not do that!"

There is no big corporation to absorb the loss, no slick corporate accountants to work out an advantage. To effectively write off shrinkage takes meticulous bookkeeping into already complicated year-end taxes. I shudder to think how things could have and probably should have been done more effectively. The knowledge grew from year to year, but those are all years lost to the nearly unavoidable learning curve.

A tale of two not-so-fair maidens took place in my first year with the store. Two attractive young women came in for the sole purpose of stealing; they were beautiful, on the outside, and wanted nothing. The short one, a blonde, was bubbly and performed the role of distracting me. The second one, a very tall and well-dressed brunette, was the head of assessing which products were

29

of value to them. They confidently walked the store surveying the inventory, free from shame, free from moral conscience. The short one proceeded to pepper me with requests to see lipstick samples, creating a situation where my back would turn to retrieve the sample. After feigning interest in that sample, she requested another, then another, essentially creating a slick tag teamed effort; she distracted while her counterpart stole. The tall thief would boldly and intermittently show a product to the short one looking for a nod of approval, which she received each time. Then they left without buying anything. They left? It was only my first few months of business with my shiny new store! I proudly presented samples and smiled. Then, with some confusion, I walked over to the area the tall one had lingered in, and there it was, empty shelves. She not only took a few items; she took stacks of the most expensive items. Not only was this store owner out of the stolen product, but she was now forced to shell out additional money for security cameras.

A police officer clarified what I pretty much already knew about my rights during a brief and blunt discussion. He explained, with a slightly defeated tone of voice, that the laws didn't exactly favor store owners. He let me know that a shoplifter has the rights, basically all the rights, until they have exited the store. Technically they can fill their backpack or duffle bag and drag it around the store. By law, they haven't shoplifted until they've walked out of the store, making the logistics of an official arrest difficult at best. But there's more than one way to skin a cat.

The magician is the nickname given to a seemingly harmless older woman who was probably in her late 70's. She browsed the store, particularly a few specific items, then left without buying anything. The employee noticed that the bracelet she was looking at simultaneously disappeared upon her departure. Boldly following her out to her car, my employee asks the customer to pay for the bracelet. After the woman denies any wrongdoing, the employee shrewdly jots down her license plate number to invite concern. It worked. A not-so-mysterious occurrence takes place when the license plate number is written down. She comes back into the store and says, "See, it's right here." She walks away, and it disappears, she comes back, hovers, it reappears!" Magic.

There were cheats and sneaks and thieves
An abundance of tricks up their sleeves
The deals weren't enough
They stole handfuls of stuff
And found numerous ways to deceive

The magician and the maidens were expected, and although I hoped I wouldn't cross paths with them, the assumption was that I would. Making matters worse is the number of people who are either oblivious to how their actions are indeed thievery or don't care. Maybe a sense of entitlement overshadows any thought of the impact on a business, or more likely, it's the assumption that any store can absorb losses here and there. But, with varying degrees of attitude from boldness to a tail in-between their legs, they leave their mark with inevitable damage.

Let's make a deal was a game that played out surprisingly often. A tester sat out for almost every item in the store, for every color and scent. Still, customers would break the seal on new packaging to see for themselves what's in the box. I'm not Monty Hall or Wayne Brady, and this isn't Let's Make a Deal, where box number one has something different from box number two. Very rarely will they ask, and they'll inevitably tear the packaging in the process. They then nonchalantly put the damaged box back on the shelf. Predictably, the next customer sees the broken packaging, deems it defective, and there it sits and eventually ends up as a loss. When witnessing them in action, I'd skulk over and state the obvious. It's a little weird to address another adult regarding what I thought was common sense. Other times they'll see me catching a glimpse of what they're doing, and they'll proceed with a slow and stealthy return of the broken box, turning it on its' side to conceal the damage, just like little kids. Those little rascals.

The odd behaviors prompted a display shelf in my office. This shelf, nicknamed "the great wall of shame," displayed products bearing peculiar but funny stories. First, there's the near-empty bottle of perfume returned because the customer didn't like it; did she have to use it so much? My crown jewel was a bottle of really old insect repellent made by the company I represented. The color was very much yellow/brown (it's supposed to be clear), which no doubt now attracted bugs. The bottle, dated 1987, was still used by its' owner in 2016 when I convinced her that it was probably time for a new one. Next, there's an EMPTY bottle of bubble bath that caused irritation, to which I say, "One CAPFUL per bath, not one BOTTLE." Also displayed is a partially unwrapped lipstick, one of two that were for sale but brazenly unwrapped by a customer like tootsie rolls. She put them back with the other inventory as I walked over to inform her on how broken seals kill any chance of selling those items. She mumbled with glassy eyes, "They were already open." I make it a habit not to mess with people with glassy eyes; I turned and slinked away. Lastly is some makeup that was returned but, in her words, only used a little bit. We heard it ALL the time over the years. There is no sales area for items used a little bit, and it's no less painful to hand their money back. Though the damaged packaging and returns were annoying, my great wall of shame was an outlet for my sarcasm and made me chuckle when walking by it throughout the years.

I was the proverbial fly on the wall on several occasions as shoplifters attempted to use my little store as a safe haven. The only good thing was that it wasn't my store that had suffered the losses. One day, two younger women come in the door and shop while attempting to look run-of-the-mill. Their attempt looked awkward and forced, so I sensed something was up. One picks up an inexpensive lip balm and walks to the register while a police officer walks in the door. Having just finished shoplifting a few doors down, they ducked into my store, attempting to avoid the police. While ringing up the lip balm, the police officer casually walked over to my paying customer and calmly handcuffed her. Slowly pushing her change across the counter, knowing full well she could no longer use her hands to pick it up, it was not a run-of-the-mill transaction. Do I say, "thank you?"

It happened on a different day with a different shoplifter, but this time she asked to store her huge tote bag filled with stolen goods near the checkout. It seemed a little out of the ordinary, but, ok. Minutes later, a police officer arrives, quickly catches on to her stash that's overflowing its' tote near the checkout, and again arrests my customer. For whatever reason, my store had become a haven. I felt like a mother hen with troubled little chicks running under my wing. "Hey, leave her alone!"

Lastly, there are the thieves of time and reputation. Although small store owners can give that extra bit of attention, that's where we shine; we're often taken advantage of with unrealistic expectations. If we're not agreeable with even unreasonable requests, we find ourselves at the mercy of the dreaded internet feedback.

A potential customer contacted me at home and asked if a product had a specific ingredient. After calling the store, I promptly asked the employee to look at the ingredient list and determine that it was not in the product. I let my customer know this, and she immediately fired back with, "Can you take a picture and send it? Thanks!" While giving her credit for saying thanks, my question is, "you have the answer, so one, why do you need a picture and two, how much time am I supposed to invest in this, quite literally, $1.99 hand cream?" My husband piped up in the background, interrupting my grumbling with, "Would she call a larger store and ask them to send her a picture of a product?" No, they would quickly deflect her question with the fallback answer, "That information is available on the internet." And that would only happen if they answered the phone, which isn't likely. As a small business owner, I'll stumble over furniture, the dog, and anything else in my way when the business phone rings. If a customer has a question that needs an answer, it's taken quite seriously. Yet, if I were to rip a page out of the playbook from the big box stores, and deliver a harsh response, then the time she could have spent researching the product on the internet would, in turn, be spent researching how to leave negative feedback for me. Anger brought on from even the most insignificant offense is a powerful motivator.

My hat is off to the uniquely talented group of people who manage to steal both time and product; well done! On occasion, I offered samples in the form of mini lipstick tubes. However, they added up quickly if someone wants to try more than a few with no real intention of purchasing a lipstick. Sometimes I'll spend 30-45 minutes pulling out, discussing, and offering samples, all the while bursting at the seams to scream out, "Just buy the $5 lipstick already!" As drops of sweat form, finding comfort in my slow but ever-growing tolerance was the saving grace. It wasn't a good day for this group when I decided to eliminate the relatively costly samples. The adage you have to spend money to make money didn't ring true for these adorable samples. I could finally relax and reply with "sorry" to the question, "Aww, no more mini lipsticks?" when deciding to discontinue those cute little buggers.

Always worrisome are the customers who browse for 30 minutes to an hour. They inevitably carry a bulky purse or tote, often gaping open with the zipper undone and always with a maze of contents that can easily conceal anything that falls in. I can't do anything but stand there and watch and watch. There might be paperwork to do, a shipment to unpack, but their unzipped tote is screaming, "If it looks like a duck, swims like a duck, and quacks like a duck, then it probably is a duck."

Their purse may be open to access their phone versus having ill intent. However, there's a fine line between trusting people and being a schmuck. I've found it's a rare occurrence that this type of customer purchases much, if anything. Then, after 45 minutes of watching while trying to look like I'm not watching, they leave without a purchase. I've not only lost the time but I'm left wondering how much product walked out with them. If a second customer walks in while I'm trying to watch Ms. Big Tote Bag, the ability to watch them is gone.

My expectations regarding theft revolved primarily around my work in retail decades earlier, in my mid-teens. The looks on my supervisors' faces spoke volumes when they found stacks of empty anti-theft plastic cases from music cassette tapes. (If you're under the age of 30, and the reference to cassette tapes has you scratching your head, ask your parents to explain.) My mindset and fairly calming attitude in owning a small store versus the much larger variety store was "small store equals small chance of theft."

The reality is that there's a lot more to theft than the five-fingered discount. In some cases, it's a simple misunderstanding of the underlying costs a small business owner undertakes. Each offense wasn't a personal attack on my store or me. I did what I could when I could; it was another cost of doing business.

"Learning to heel with patience and self-control"

Chapter 5
Obedience Class

In order to properly perform my duties as a store owner, I needed to go to obedience class. I would learn to heel with patience and self-control. I would learn to be quiet instead of barking and fetch when people pointed. And if things got hairy with an alpha dog, or worse yet, a cat, I learned to roll over and wag my tail. It wasn't in my nature, but I learned to be a gooood girl.

Bending over backwards to accrue
Pleasant comments from a good review
Saying the wrong thing
Will certainly bring
A low rating and lost revenue

Most transactions are uneventful, but returns are a grey area; the customer is already disappointed on some level. And from the store owner's perspective, the wound from handing back money is coupled with the temperamental ground of balancing rules with kind words. Thus, always mindful of online reviews and comments, my responses had to be laced with caution.

A lady eyeballing the purchase of a $4.99 lip gloss asked, "If I don't like the shade, can I return this?" to which I cheerfully replied, "of course!" Another customer, sporting what had to be a 30 or 40-pound purse, arrived with several broken items. She said, "Your products are guaranteed, right, even for the packaging?" Of course!

39

Just because my day starts with a few bucks doesn't mean it can't be erased with the dreaded bag of returns. That's what I think every time a customer approaches the store, holding a bag. My tail droops as I see them walk through the door.

The most common and expensive returns are from anti-aging products when they don't produce a miracle. One of my repeat offenders would buy, briefly try, and ultimately return one anti-aging crème after another. She was only in her 30's, had beautiful skin, but was frustrated with the whole idea of aging at all. I wanted to tell her that "Nothing will make you look 20, except being 20." Regrettably, my advice usually went by the wayside when reminding her not to expect miracles but rather a subtle but noticeable difference. And, I could count on seeing her a month later when she'd bring them back and start the process over with a slightly different product carrying a slightly different promise.

The most memorable and somewhat amusing return was from a woman who came in looking to replace her face powder, old as dirt and ironically resembling dirt. Amazingly the name of the color on the bottom of the container was still legible: translucent. My eyebrows raised as I processed the name versus the actual color, a formerly whitish powder now the color of cocoa tainted with years of skin oils, filth, and germs. Eew While handing her a shiny new translucent powder, she abruptly says, "No, that's not the right color." Knowing the battle was probably already lost, yet feeling some responsibility to say something, I used safe words like "a little", "maybe" and "I think." I said, "You know, yours is a little older. Maybe the color has darkened quite a bit on it," only to be countered with "Oh no, I'm sure it's this one, I'm sure of it." She chose Mocha. Ok, one last-ditch attempt. "I think that one may be way too dark. I'm quite sure yours is translucent, the lightest one in the line; how about we try something in between?" Nope, hellbent on one of the darkest in the line, which, true enough, did look a lot like her biology experiment, she proceeded with her purchase and went on her way. Within two weeks, she was back returning Mocha and telling me, as if I never warned her, "I bought this, and the girl (I think we know who the girl was) who sold it to me got me the wrong color; this is waaay too dark."

My hat is off to the big-hearted people who make a genuine effort to take the time to leave an honest and yet positive review on social media. After all, a happy customer doesn't have a fire lit under them and is far less likely to make an effort than our disgruntled friends. I've been fortunate to receive, for the most part, good reviews for my small business. Each time I found one posted, I felt thankful and somewhat indebted. It affects the reputation and subsequent sales, and it's an easy (and free) gift to give a business. As a patron of restaurants, campgrounds, and hotels, "the little guys" vulnerability is all too clear. I, too, pay attention to reviews and quickly pass over those who are, well, not looking too good.

Fortunately, my potential customer base was unlikely to review or rely on online comments if a negative review came along. However, because of my personal feelings on the subject, I'm drawn to and intrigued by comments left on more vulnerable businesses, like restaurants and hotels. I've read a lot of reviews and shouldn't be so surprised (but I am) at the boldness of people. The ease of anonymity of social media is unfortunate, and I'm relieved when I'm not in their shoes.

A quick google search yielded a few examples of actual reviews for various restaurants and hotels, complete with the dreaded one-star ratings. One restaurant patron simply said "I feel sorry for them, one star." Apparently, they didn't feel sorry enough to leave constructive criticism. Another said they "can get better food at a gas station." Witty. Yet another stated "View was fantastic, food was average, 1 star." Seems a bit harsh. And as for hotels, they're prime targets. "This place should be demolished, one star." Tell us what you really think! "One star is too high, needs a negative rating system." Wow, ouch! Reading several reviews from ocean-front hotels really drove home unrealistic expectations. They complained about too many rocks and too much seaweed on the beach…it's AN OCEAN!

Though I've received far more positive internet feedback than negative, it's hard to stay on your toes all the time and impossible to be perfect. With any problems come potential solutions for a price.

Crawling out from the woodwork come those who look to profit from your misfortune. They began to fill my business mailbox with flyers promising to fix any existing and forthcoming lousy review for a fee, yet another charge. "Our software can improve your rankings!" and "Angry customers are far more vocal than satisfied customers, we can help!" were a few of their promises. Yeah, I'm well aware of how a bad review looks but can't afford to pay another bill. They would say my business can't afford not to, to which I would reply, "No, it really can't take on another bill."

I realized that a little pro-active action might be in order to help offset any forthcoming hand grenades. So, with the help of my much younger employee, who was hardwired to figure these computer things out, we devised (ok, she devised) a paragraph of instructions that described how to leave feedback on several different sites on the internet. That way, we could hand it out to a customer we felt would make the effort to leave a kind but still genuine comment. We had regular customers that we knew were pleased with our service, and they told us all the time. Since anger is such a powerful motivator, seeking out satisfied customers seemed necessary. I've been asked to do it myself while checking out at hotels and am now more than happy to help out a fellow business owner with positive but still honest feedback.

The first time I ran across a negative comment, though almost inevitable, was disturbing. Unless you have no feelings, it's a jolt. It'd been sitting there for over six months before I discovered it, which left me in a dilemma; should it be addressed after all this time? Wouldn't that be like picking off a scab? So, it lay there, unaddressed and screaming incompetence since I wasn't looking. It didn't even occur to me that I was a candidate for one, but it's impossible to be perfect.

Amidst clear anger, this person gave quite a description of not one but two employees who were seemingly laughing at video footage from the security cameras. She assumed, incorrectly I believe, they were laughing at customers. Instead, they were likely laughing at a staff member, probably me, who tends to dance when I'm by myself. That didn't exactly put my mind at ease.

In all honesty, it could have even been me the customer saw laughing, as I've shown coworkers video clips while (very) nervously laughing about scary situations that have arisen during my shifts. I specifically remember catching the sight of a customer, giving me the stink eye during one such occasion. I broke a fundamental rule: never laugh in the presence of other people if they could interpret it the wrong way.

By piecing together comments from staff, it was evident that videos were inappropriately viewed. There were too many partial stories that made me ask, "How would she know that?" In addition, it was upsetting that the liberties allowed with open passwords were taken lightly. It never occurred to me that it would have ever been an issue, but sadly the password was changed and kept to myself.

On a lighter and more awkward note, adding to my bone-chilling realization of privacy issues was the fact that I love to dance, that is when I'm alone or think I'm alone. One of the highlights of my working by myself and alongside a terrific sound system is that I'm dancing, free of shame, and free of talent when there are no customers. While I would never enthusiastically dance in public, I felt pretty comfortable and irrationally confident that my dancing wasn't half bad. Additionally, I thought the motion activated security cameras kept to themselves; that's going to haunt me for a while. In addition to the cameras, there are large plate glass windows in the front of the store. Come to find out, windows are see-through; I was reminded of this the day I was dancing, out of control really, to a Bee Gees song. After catching sight of two women walking in, my confidence ended abruptly as their fixated eyes and smirks confirmed my fears. It jerked me out of my overly comfortable little world.

Expectations regarding store reviews and keeping customers happy lined up with reality. I would be on my best behavior (usually) when it came to returns, complaints and requests. And those prayers for patience churned out over the years? They were answered in the form of a lot of practice.

"Hey there little store, you just keep trying, it's so cute to watch"

Chapter 6
The Little Guy

One of the biggest surprises of owning a small store was realizing just how different it was to be up close and personal with almost every customer. It created exciting conversations and intriguing insight, not only in their interactions with staff but in how they viewed the little guy and their store. Everything from price increases to personal space was different in the small store setting.

Separating my little store from the larger chain stores, I've found, is a double-edged sword. Shoppers understand that a small store comes with a more personal service, and I tried my best to provide it. On the other hand, a few too many believe that since they're no longer dealing with a large store with long-established rules carved in stone, well, perhaps they can use this to their advantage. The burden of convincing them that, yes, rules still apply was very real. My overhead and inventory costs leave me with very little wiggle room on price and no cushion to cut prices on a whim. I found myself apologizing for standard and inevitable markups. My presence as the owner, stock boy, janitor, cashier, and complaint department made me fair game.

It was often assumed that I make up prices as I go along or raise and lower them at will. It's pretty straightforward for the little guy; we buy the product, add a standard markup, and, yeah, that's the price. The problem is, as prices rise, so does the frequency of complaints. After directing a customer to a face product with a current sale price of $8.99, she loudly exclaims, "Oh my gosh! Last time I only paid $6.00 each, and I bought five of them; OH MY GOSH!" As the little guy, I'd find myself dealing with and explaining decisions from the parent company, decisions that in no way involved me.

The perfect storm came when corporate not only doubled the price of a product but cut its' contents in half simultaneously. I knew I was in for it. One of my regulars came in, discovered the blow, and looked at me with a look of horror twirled with a saddening pain. She shouted, "$7.99?!" quickly followed by an empty stare and a second but much more lethargic comment, "But mine is twice the size."

I delivered my standard apology with a subdued sincerity, "I'm sorry, sometimes these things happen." It was almost as if I was a preacher trying to explain an untimely death, natural disaster, or disease instead of the price hike on a stick of blush. She followed with not one but two more redundant statements, but by now with a limp voice as this first world problem had destroyed hers, "Mine is twice the size, it's... twice the size."

Straight-up haggling wasn't unheard of, and I had to learn to deal with them tactfully. Some are upfront, "Will you take less for this?" as though it's a flea market. Even worse, I've been so boldly asked multiple times, "Do you have anything for free?" It's the samples this group seeks, and a lot of them, finding it not only cost-efficient but fun as they gloss over my expense. Some inform me of their upcoming vacation and would like as many samples as can be spared. Absolutely!

Others try to guilt you into keeping products marked at whatever their all-time lowest sale price was, forever. I'm not out to get anyone. I'm just trying to pay my bills and walk away with a few bucks to spare. And unlike most stores where workers are like mice, scattering in the presence of people, I was in plain sight and made for an easy target.

One customer came in for underarm deodorant that had been on sale for years for a mere 99 cents. When the new sale price became $1.75, I then became a target for his frustration. I stood behind the shelter of my counter and held on. After complaining about the price multiple times, and my trying to explain the price hike numerous times, he angrily thumped his deodorants on the counter. It almost seemed like a scene out of a sitcom. He then added, in case I didn't get the point, that he wouldn't be back. It was a relief because the price went up again by another 50% just months after that. Thankfully an angel of sorts was sent literally the next day, ironically another guy, who happily plopped down multiple deodorants and said, "I love these things; they're priceless." He used those words verbatim, and I thought to myself, "Wow, that was weird." The Ying and the Yang had paid me a visit that week. Of all the things I thought I'd experience in the store, "cosmic duality" wasn't one of them.

Shop small to support the little guy
As long as the prices are low, not high
A sale guarantee
Or better yet free
Or else they'll be saying goodbye

The most contradictory objection happened on a semi-regular basis and played out something like this: Customer carrying a $400 purse asks about a small cosmetics item, "Why is this $3.99? It's normally on sale for $1.99." The challenge came in trying to answer in a calm voice while hypnotically glaring at the expensive handbag. But, the power of online reviews always kept me in line. I'm at the parent company's mercy, so the answer is simple: it's priced according to what I pay. And in spite of the posh handbag, the matching wallet, the outrageously expensive shoes, or some combination thereof, I internalized any looming parental type lecture.

I admit that a bad precedence was set as a green and somewhat desperate store owner in my first few years. I quickly reduced prices on every impulse request. Basing my spineless actions on the saying that a happy customer is a loyal customer, over time, it was clear that it never felt right to lower the price "just because." It caused me to feel as though what I was selling wasn't worth the total amount, even though I knew full well, my products were both of quality and already at rock bottom prices.

The confidence slowly came to calmly explain, rather than apologize, that a standard markup is applied to the inventory based on cost. Still, I would get the occasional look like I'M the unreasonable one. However, I am comforted from time to time from the customers who do understand and validate with "Well, you can't help the price increases your company sets." Bless their hearts.

She jumped through the hoops that were there
Creating a store with some flair
But often was dazed
Her eyebrows were raised
In handling people with care

Being careful became an artform in this up close and personal world. The one question that presented itself more often than it rightly should have, and the one that made my toes curl, was, "How old do I look?" It was always said with a smile and proud assertion, and really, how else can one reply? I can hardly spit out my real guess for fear of guessing too high, and even a perfect guess would be a disappointment for them. So, after sizing them up and knocking a good 10-15 years off of my answer, I'd blurt out, "Well, I'd say the mid to late fifties?" with a serious tone, furrowed brow, and pursed lips. Very much satisfied with the answer, their smile grows into a full-blown toothy grin, then bursting at the seams, they yell "70!" While cringing on the inside, the awkward exchange finishes with, "Really! You're kidding!" Like an animal backed into a corner, I see no other way to handle the situation. Another much younger customer witnessed this swapping of weirdness and asked me,

"How often does THAT happen?" I honestly replied, "way more often than I'd like." In all fairness, some of them really were aging well. I'd sometimes be blown away at their fantastic genes, but no, I don't want to guess ANYONE'S age.

Once I indeed did slip up after suggesting a cologne to a gentleman that seemed to be around 55 years old. After he requested a cologne suggestion, I foolishly said, "This is our best-selling cologne, usually for guys over 50." D'oh! Although it was well-intentioned, he did NOT like the suggestion that he had fallen into the "guys over 50" category. His feathers were ruffled, and he reminded me of my failure more than once. He strolled the store with his wife, intermittently injecting the phrase "since I'm over 50" into every comment. Chill out; it's not like I guessed high!

To put things in perspective, first, I'm a girl of the eighties. The funny thing is, I put that cologne into the fifty-plus category the day a twenty-something-year-old came into the store. He too asked for a cologne suggestion, and my reply was, "this is our best-selling men's cologne," and held it out for him to take a whiff. I graduated high school in the eighties, love all things from the eighties, including the smells. This was clearly an eighties smell. The second the aroma hit his youthful nose, he recoiled and shouted, "Eew! It smells like an old man!" WELL! Apparently, I'm attracted to old men because I found the smell delightful. However, it did teach me a thing or two about age groups, likes, and dislikes. The first guy, the FIFTY-FIVE-year-old, led me to show a little restraint while speculating ages, even if it is spot on.

Another regular customer who was 60 years old has striking olive skin. Her beautiful accent suggests she is from South America, and she's one of the lucky ones that won big with her "genetic scratch-off lottery ticket." We all get one, and we unknowingly scratch them off in our forties or fifties. Yes, she takes care of her skin, but she's also inclined to favor far fewer aging issues like age spots.

I'm as washed-out as they come and unfortunately burnt myself regularly in my youth; it's payback time for me. I had a "what is going on?" moment when approaching age 50 as age spots, skin tags, and barnacles began popping up like weeds. I rubbernecked when my dermatologist casually told me I had barnacles. Barnacles? It's bad news because they can't be picked off (I've tried), and they are as unattractive as it sounds. After asking him to please remove my barnacles, skin tags, and age spots, he dared to ask, "What exactly are you calling age spots, and why are you calling them age spots?" Really? I'll tell you why. It's because my friend asked me, as only a friend can, about all of the mushrooming age spots on my hands. His question was ripe with untethered bluntness as he simply asked, "What's the deal with your hands?" I couldn't google "local dermatologist" fast enough.

The good news is, my skin helps me relate when someone comes in and asks me to work miracles. One customer vividly sticks out; she made a difficult request during my fledging first year in business. She was quite a bit older, and the skin above her eyelids was badly sagging over her eyelids. The well-defined folds of skin suggested not only normal aging but simple, and sometimes unfortunate, genetics. She asked me with both hopefulness and seriousness, "Do you have any creams that would help this?" There have been moments I've been speechless; that was one of them.

Creams have their place, but I'm not a liar and wasn't going to start then. With honesty, I replied, "Creams might help a little, but there's just not much you can do." She seemed a little disappointed that no such miracle cream existed, but, in hindsight, I handled the situation very wrong. Though correct in offering honesty, I should have at the same time provided a product that may have made her FEEL better. Without raiding her wallet, a "dose of feel-good" in a jar may have lifted her spirits without making any miracle claims.

This line of work has brought with it insight; there's a lot more to retail than merely selling products. People's feelings and self-esteem come into play. The responsibility to be careful and gentle when stepping into their world shouldn't be taken lightly. And then there are other times that I try and step into their world, and they're just not having it...

Bacteria Smacteria is a motto, a way of life really, learned from a customer who began a conversation with, "How long are lipsticks good?" My quick yet sensible response was, "If they remain sealed, about two years, but once you start using them, six months to a year." She replied, "I've had mine a while; they have an odor that wasn't there when they were new." I respond, "If they've developed an odor, it's time for them to go." Unbelievably she continues, "Why?" Entertaining her odd question with yet another rational answer: "If they've developed an odor, they're crawling with bacteria, you need to get rid of them." Holding her ground, she says, "But how do I know it'll hurt me? Can't I keep using them?" After a quick scan for a candid camera, I quickly accessed my alibi, the internet, to quote some common sense since my prudent advice was not getting through to bacteria woman. I quote, "It says here old makeup is a breeding ground for all sorts of creepy infections. Makeup that contains water, which they almost all do, are at a higher risk because water provides bacteria a friendly little home." Not the answer she wanted, she gave me the "whatever" look and continued, without a new $5 lipstick.

Some motherly advice came MY way in a no-nonsense statement from yet another helpful customer. I've been on the receiving end of guidance and validation by merely being surrounded by my own kind. Although women can be catty, shockingly so, they have their moments offering validation as only one woman can to another woman…

One day I was eavesdropping on a conversation between two women several years older than myself; they were on a roll complaining about their health. Chiming in with MY new and developing age and weight-related problems, one of them strolled over to me much as a parent would to deliver, "the talk." She said, "Honey, it all goes downhill after age 55. How old are you?" I replied, "55." With a look that said uh-huh, she stepped closer, to sum up her point with yet more brutal honesty and said, "Get used to it; it blows." Well, ok then.

I've had numerous exchanges with strangers that want to be heard, and it's been a blessing. I've been both honored to be there for them and that they trust me with their personal stories of loss and other burdens. I've never considered myself an approachable person, and it's made me feel human to know that a few people think that I am. It's been a pleasure to have people remember my name, call me by name, and vice versa. These exchanges and relaxed friendships have been unexpected and welcome. It's been a pleasant secondary effect of being a little guy. Author Randy Pausch said, "When we're connected to others, we become better people." He may be right.

My expectations were that I was capable of going above and beyond an average small store. Much like the well-organized garage sales I held for years, the rewards would be reaped with few issues while maintaining a detached persona. My comfortable and somewhat isolated world had a safe zone, and I preferred staying in it.

The reality was that I would find a challenge with most everything in this new setting of a small retail business. I needed to "wake up" and leave my safe zone to connect with people rather than detach. My customers chose my little store over the big box store option for a reason, which was everything exactly opposite of a disengaged store owner. What began as annoying habits of people became full of character and life. It felt like the scene in the Wizard of Oz when everything went from black and white to color, and "seeing" people became an unexpected gift.

"Onesies oksies, twosies go awaysies"

Chapter 7
A Onesies and a Twosies

The image a small business portrays is essential and sets us apart from the giants. For example, after trying hard to create a spa for retail shopping, I received hundreds if not thousands of comments over the decade like, "I love this little store," "thank you for being here," and my personal favorite, "I want to relax in those chairs, I don't want to go home." It was appreciated, and it validated the effort. The small stores are holding the one card that large retailers cannot, personal service. A clean bathroom, lounge chairs, and a sympathetic ear concerning weight gain, sagging skin, and "batwing" arms round off the experience. I framed jokes that women could appreciate and hung them in unsuspecting places accented with greenery. Comfortable leather chairs, an ottoman, and reading material sat at the far end of the store. Beyond that was a bathroom decorated with framed photos of heartthrob men and a cute curio cabinet.

Using the bathroom was a pleasure. Any woman can testify, a clean and inviting public restroom is a rare and treasured thing. I had a reputation for my bathroom, which I learned over time, really isn't a good thing. A woman came into the store with a quick and purposeful waddle blurting out during her funny walk that she had "held it" until she got to my store. Other women would grab their friends and say, "You have to see this bathroom, even if you don't have to go; I feel better just having walked in there!" That made me smile, but then

59

there were the others. I've had way too many women set up camp in there and have had to go knock on the door to ask, "Everything ok?" hoping to speed along the process and avoid the inevitable meandering cloud.

My husband and I devised the perfect wording for a sign that read "Onesies OKsies, twosies, go awaysies." We never found the boldness to hang it, but it became an ongoing joke. On the other hand, I sometimes have to break my own rules and partake in the twosies; after all, I sometimes work 9+ hour shifts. Anyone who works in close proximity to other people can probably relate…

The twosies can be a real problem in certain jobs. I try to be quick about it, but there's nothing fast with a woman going to the bathroom as any woman can testify.

I've been caught on several occasions, but one such ill-timed afternoon still makes my eye twitch. After four to five minutes, success was achieved, which seemed reasonable enough, but I also successfully nuked the bathroom; it shocked even me. While washing my hands, the doorbell dings from an incoming customer. Emerging while at the same time spraying air fresheners, the bathroom door was closed with astonishing speed. I tried to play it cool. I leave the bathroom and simultaneously cross paths with a dude on a mission and beelining towards it. What did I do to deserve this?! Caught seriously off guard, honesty seemed to be my only option. I could only think fast enough to say to him in a desperate panic, "You're playing with fire if you go in there!" I was completely serious, but he didn't heed my warning but instead entered into the cloud, much like a well-used campground bathroom, the kind that makes you say, "You gotta be kidding me." Trying to disguise the odor with multiple air fresheners (I kept four in there), only made it worse. Doused with humility, I stood at the cash register, trying to pretend everything was normal while wondering what kind of look this guy would be wearing when he came out of there, but of course, it couldn't end there. As soon as he came out, his wife went in (why not?!). When she came out, there was a hushed discussion of which I could only hear him saying "no," to which she undoubtedly had asked, "Did you do that?" When awkward moments have arisen in the past, I'm generally on top of my game and will work in lies that usually begin with "The customer that was just in here..."

You're probably wondering about now, "enough with the bathroom, when is she going to stop talking about the bathroom?" but unfortunately, there's more. Though challenging to top the dude that beelined into my bat cave, I had to discuss bathroom etiquette with not one but two different customers. They made a second home and spent upwards of 30 minutes or longer in the bathroom on a very regular basis. They would walk into the store and instantaneously ask, "Can I use your bathroom?" while I resisted screaming, "NO!" Speaking with sensitive phrases like "it's understandable" and "a little unsuitable," they thankfully received it without offense. I also found that it wasn't just the products in the store that were ripe for theft; so were bathroom items, including the liquid soap and even the nightlight. I went in there for my moment of Zen after closing, and it was like, "Hey! Where's my nightlight?!"

All joking aside, an overly used bathroom in a small space is not a good thing when you're trying to sell beauty products. There was one other noteworthy day when a young customer spent a bit too long in the bathroom...

The elusive and rare tampon plant (sanguiferous corkus arborus) blooms but once every eight years, and it was my lucky day. On that day, a grandmother came in with her 11-year-old granddaughter. She asked if there was a bathroom that her granddaughter could use, and I pointed her to the right door. After the granddaughter closed the door, her grandmother veered her attention to me, lowered her voice, and said, "You know, she just got her period." With some awkwardness, I responded with, "Wow, that IS young." Then grandma told me SHE didn't get her period until she was 13, yet more information I didn't need to know. After almost chiming in with the age my period began, I stopped myself, but smiled. It reminded me of one of my husbands' favorite lines, "put a couple of women in a room and within two minutes they'll be talking about their periods." Anyways, after way too long in the bathroom, grandma remarks, "What the heck is taking her so long in there?" Shortly afterward, we witness the emergence of the granddaughter promenading out with a confident bounce in her step. A few hours later, at closing time, I locked the door, counted my drawer, then headed to the bathroom, where I perched comfortably on my porcelain stool and breathed in a sigh of relief. Ahhh. It's only after closing time that I can truly relax on the toilet without the fear of hearing the all too certain ding of the doorbell. During this moment of relaxation, my eyes became fixated on the plant in front of me. On this plant, I spotted where granddaughter took it upon herself to unwrap an extra tampon to hang on the fake plant directly in front of the toilet. She cleverly wound it in-between the stems as though it belonged to and was growing on the plant. Maybe I was a bit too tired or perhaps regressed, just for a moment, to when I too was 11 years old, but the scene just struck me as funny, really funny. I couldn't stop laughing for a good five minutes. I was still chuckling after walking out the door to my car.

It's been both funny and, at times, heartbreaking to be there. A smaller environment offers a haven for those who need to talk. A death in the family or ongoing cancer treatments put life in perspective. I'm honored to lend an ear. It also presented optimal conditions for all manner of conversation. Oddly enough, questions about the weather and medical problems frequently came my way as though I had some specialized knowledge. The funny thing was that when delivering my answer, they looked at me, nodding their head and stroking their chin with this weird admiration. Was it my being a store owner that bumped me up a notch? Was it selling products for women? Who knows, but I was careful not to overstep my bounds. I often quoted the internet, followed by, "But you'll probably want to check with your doctor."

Being a store primarily for women was cause for plenty of corroborating about hormone problems, weight gain, and, of course, men. I witnessed sneaky little schemes like paying part of the bill in cash and part on credit to hide the bill in its' entirety. Several women had husbands linger in the store, probably to minimize the damage. It was humorous to watch the interactions between them. I smiled as a woman was paying her bill while her husband walked in, and I quietly asked, "Does he belong to you?" She responded with a VERY disappointed "yeah." They often cautioned me, "you just wait until YOUR husband retires." Bearing witness to my own kind surprised even me. We can be nasty little creatures.

My expectations of the stores' personal space were minimal. You're probably wondering, "did you put much thought into any of this?" to which I'd honestly say, "not really, but I think that may have been a good thing."

In reality, it's possible to be too prepared. Had I known about every stressful moment, or heard every prayer I blubbered through, I would never have proceeded. George Bernard Shaw said, "A life spent making mistakes is not only more honorable but more useful than a life spent doing nothing."

"Come again? A what kind of tax?"

Chapter 8
What the FUTA?

When I set up my business banking account, the banker confidently and without flinching said, "Business accounts are free here." The angels sang, and I thought to myself, "That's terrific!" But as time marched on, I would reply to his statement as Jim Carey so accurately summed up things by saying, "reheheheally!"

We started noticing charges on our account that ranged anywhere from 33 cents to $15. They were stealthy about it, but over time these charges increased in amount and consistency. They were labeled with three intentionally vague words, analysis service charges. I called the bank to get an expanded explanation and was greeted with a recording that funneled me to their website. Unwilling to get online and set up yet another portal and password, I drove to the bank to decipher this anomaly.

I requested an audience with a bank specialist, sat down at her desk, and began to probe. I was armed with sarcasm and distrust regarding anything that raided my little bank account. She winced a bit before proceeding to give me the "please don't shoot the messenger" look. She explained that the bulk of the charges were for depositing partial cash instead of all charge card payments. Furthermore, the bank charged me every time I requested rolled coins or larger bills were exchanged for smaller ones. The bottom line, cash is no longer king, and small businesses get nailed whether they accept cash or credit. The credit card companies take their percent immediately; the bank takes the rest every time you deposit cash, ask for cash, or mention the word cash. My initial assumption that the bank would be delighted with getting my small business account was beginning to fade. An IRS auditor once said, "the trick is to stop thinking of it as 'your' money." I was starting to understand; it seems far more time is spent earning money for other people than for the business itself.

For years I wondered if government agencies really check due dates against postmarks. They do. The state is calculating and shrewd; they have a tripwire of sorts that got me several years into my business. Sometimes, your payment is due on the 20th of the month, and sometimes it's due on the last day of the month. And once a year, it's due on the 19th, pow, zing! I was caught in their snare after mailing my monthly retail taxes and paperwork ONE DAY LATE. My penance included a $100 fine for one lousy day. My husband laughed and said, "I bet they have a bell they ring when they find one!"

I fumbled my way through the paperwork for retail taxes but hired out payroll and all of its' related taxes and forms. Now partially out of the loop, I randomly signed documents as they emerged from my accountant. I could've been signing most anything. When I DO take it upon myself to tackle government paperwork or, worse yet, phone calls, patience never was one of my virtues.

68

One such day had me trying to accomplish two tasks with the state department of revenue. First, I needed to update my mailing address and then request a new payment voucher booklet (one that, for the record, still hadn't arrived TWO YEARS later). Before making the call, I obediently got online and created a portal, my new most despised word. After inventing yet another cumbersome username, I answered three security questions while gritting my teeth at the thought of putting more personal information online. Unfortunately, what little enthusiasm I had did a U-turn after discovering the website would not accomplish what I thought. So…

I'm forced to call the State Department of Revenue. After weaving through the first set of automated questions, I select a number with uncertainty. I say uncertainty because every option is attached to an overly lengthy description that could disorientate most any caller. By the time it gets to option ten, all I'm thinking is, "seven sounded kind of like it, but maybe it was option three, or was it four?" After selecting a number, I'm blasted with another set of ten options. Really? Clinking my imaginary glass of wine in the air, I cherry-picked another number. Then, an abrupt message blurts out, "All of our representatives are busy with other customers; please go to our website." **CLICK**, yes, click.

"Your call is important to us. Please stay on the line until your call is no longer important to you."
– online meme

I finally spoke to a human, who promised to mail a new payment voucher booklet. Several months later, when said booklet still hadn't arrived (big surprise), I sent in my payment on yet another makeshift form, an old voucher replaced with a new date. This time, however, it included a note to try and get their attention. I wrote in large letters, "pretty please with sugar on top, can I have a new payment voucher booklet with an updated mailing address," followed by a big elementary toothy hand-drawn smiley face. My husband peered over my shoulder at my artwork, and with a grim warning, said, "careful."

I did receive a response to my appeal and artwork; they incorrectly changed the business's address and not the mailing address, making matters even worse. This change improperly altered the tax rate to match the mistakenly changed business address, so I now needed to correct that AND STILL get the original task completed.

The snowball kept rolling as warning notices began to show up in the mail that my payments were hit or miss, and they were missing several. My suspicion was that my improvised payment forms were partially to blame or, God forbid, my name had made it onto some blacklist. Regardless, I dutifully produced proof of payments, including copies of canceled checks, and submitted a large packet of paperwork, everything they needed to verify payments. I smugly thought, "Wow, I bet you didn't expect me to have all of that on hand. Ha, ha, ha, who's laughing now!?" They were, and they sent a certified letter which stated I now owed late fees plus the missing payments. As for the lost ones, it was again up to me to try and prove otherwise.

Numbed with frustration, I picked up the phone and weaved through the usual maze of options ending with, "All of our representatives are busy…" Then, fully committed, I redialed, but to outsmart them, chose a different route through the mouse maze and happily found myself at number seven waiting in line. If you've seen Seinfeld's episode when George and Jerry are in line with the Soup Nazi, you can imagine my new self-control. I was now similar to a trail horse, a once spirited animal that was reluctantly obeying with my ears pricked back.

My new and improved obedience would be rewarded after a 15-minute phone call and an ah-ha moment. The voice on the other end deciphered what had happened to my payments. It turns out that re-using old payment vouchers was a terrible idea. The old coupons had a code on the bottom of them that identified payment dates. Even though I had manually crossed off old dates and replaced them with new ones, the barcode was still being scanned, applying my payments to periods long since passed. I had created a mess. The state employee told me, very nicely, that although he couldn't fix my problem over the phone, an email dialog detailing the course of events could. About six months later, an email arrived saying everything was right as rain; it was like winning the lottery. As for the payment voucher booklet, I threw in the towel and instead printed a standard, regrettably longer form off the internet. I could live with that.

Taxes from city and county and fed
Assuring the store would stay in the red
A brick-and-mortar store
Turned quickly to a chore
Of credit debt and overhead

My mind now processes all thoughts regarding employment in terms of government taxation. When we offered our teenage son $20 tax-free cash an hour to mow our lawn, and he declined in favor of working a regular job for $8 an hour, my head just about exploded. Ignoring his "oh mom" look, I tried to explain that the government would take their chunk out of his $8 per hour job, leaving him with only about $6 per hour. Instead, he could be making $20 an hour mowing our grass, tax-free! When I considered renting a space in an antique mall to sell painted furniture, one of my first questions for the merchant was, "Do you issue a 1099 form at the end of the year?" When she replied, "Yes," I was speechless before uttering the word "bummer."

They say it takes three to five years for a small business to turn a profit; they're not kidding. I'd say it's closer to five to ten years. And that only happens if you're not paying yourself much. Realistically, you can't afford help those first few years; the money isn't there. The only way we survived was because my husbands' government job supported the store. Ironic, isn't it?

My business is small; I only have four employees plus myself. Yet regardless of its' size, every government entity has latched onto a teat. As Inigo Montoya says in the movie The Princess Bride, "Let me explain, no, there is too much, let me sum up." I will attempt to sum up:

Every month, on the 15th, the IRS reaches into our account and takes out about $700. This money includes funds withheld from employee paychecks for federal income taxes plus FICA (Social Security and Medicare), a healthy 7.65% of everyone's income. Furthermore, and this is depressing, the business matches FICA; that comes straight out of the business owners' pocket. Ouch!

Every month, on the 20th, a check goes to the State Department for retail taxes, but this money was never mine to begin with. It's collected with every purchase and amounts to just over 9% of every sale. It's kindly held in my account for them until I do the math and write a sizeable check, all done out of the kindness of my heart.

For the record, I don't collect it out of the kindness of my heart, and it's a thorn in my side, "for crying out loud, don't forget the 20TH! Mine or not, I better have the money in the account to pay them on time. If I'm late, even by one day, I'm slapped with fines even though I'm doing THEM the favor of collecting taxes, hey now! Those checks range anywhere from $1200-$3000 depending on sales that month. It's really annoying to have money in your account that isn't yours.

73

Every quarter, two checks are written to the State Department. The first is for state taxes withheld from employee paychecks, and the second is the one percent of gross employee wages that I unhappily pitch in to add to the state unemployment pot.

At the end of every year, I receive several unwelcome surprises. One of them is year-end personal property taxes. That's right; in some cities and counties, you pay taxes, every year, on the stuff you already own and already paid retail taxes on, including the toilet paper, literally! It seems the minute you have a surplus, another bill comes along. Where there's a will there's a way, and we could always visit an old friend... hello 2nd mortgage!

Lastly, a rather large manilla envelope from my accountant arrives. It contains more mystery forms and money due to the Feds, but it's usually just a couple hundred dollars. Come to find out, I pay a FUTA tax.

What is a FUTA, you ask? I'll be honest; until I started writing this book I didn't even know, I just paid it. Although it sounds like something made up, it stands for the federal unemployment tax act., at least that's what Google is telling me. Employees don't pay into FUTA, but employers do, and this particular pot "funds the federal government's oversight of each state's unemployment program" as if each state can't handle it on its own. What the FUTA!

My expectations were pretty out of whack on this one, even I have to admit that. I severely underestimated the vastness and depth of taxes and government paperwork. Train wreck pretty much sums it up.

The reality is that there's a lot of taxes out there. I continually looked at my accountant like he had three heads and pushed my limits by repeatedly asking, "How's that again?"

*"Observing the small business owner
in its natural habitat…"*

Chapter 9
The Retail Hamster Wheel

Frequently people assume that just because someone owns a store, they must have money and a lot of it. I was one of them; I'm not now. Owning a small business is like being on a hamster wheel. You can run and run, you can even spin around upside down, but you aren't necessarily going to get to the legendary pot of gold.

One adverse meeting with a customer drove this home. "I know how much this store makes," were the words she growled at me. She is a customer I'd had several run-ins with over the years and was a classic illustration of a quote found on picturequotes.com. "The most unhappy people are the ones who always undervalue what they have, and overvalue what others have." Although I voluntarily gave her a discount on her purchases as she was a friend of a friend (of a friend), it was never enough. On this day, she wanted a discontinued item that I still had in stock, and she wanted it cheap.

I wasn't in the store, so she instructed my employee to sell her four bottles of the discontinued item at the outlet book clearance price of $9.99. She also wanted her regular 25% discount. Noting that the resulting amount of $7.50 was well below the posted shelf price of $30.00, the employee rightly calls me asking for direction. Keeping my employee out of the line of fire, I asked to speak with the customer:

Me: I'm sorry, those were purchased well before they went on clearance pricing. I paid the sale price of $15, which is what I'll sell them to you for, plus you can have the 25% discount, making them $11.25. My cost is $7.50, so we'd split the profit, $3.75 for me, $3.75 for you.

Her: I want the $9.99 price plus the 25% discount. I know how much this store makes.

Me: (taken aback) There's a lot of overhead with this store; I can't afford to sell things at cost unless it's necessary. I'm offering to split the profit with you.

Fit to be tied, she stomped out of the store, yelling, "I have overhead too! I have gas money AND my time!"

This wasn't my first confrontation with her, and she didn't get it, not at all. I had optimistic hopes for those remaining discontinued items. They were unusually popular, and Christmas was right around the corner. Knowing they would sell at full price on a retail shelf gave me a rare opportunity to make up for losses taken elsewhere. Selling them for more than 60% off the price I KNEW I could get seemed more than fair.

To her, I say, "Let's talk numbers." She came in on a Saturday, my biggest day of the week. My goal for a Saturday is $1000 in sales, and sometimes we make it, sometimes we don't. That's for a 9-hour day. The product's cost, coupons, clearances, and an average of 40% earnings leave the store with $400 to pay overhead.

On a typical Saturday, about $150 is spent on payroll and $100/day for rent. In a scary summary, an average Saturday brings in $1000 minus $600 for the product minus $150 for payroll minus $100 for rent leaving $150. We haven't even considered computer support, advertising, utilities, payroll taxes for employees, landscaping, snow and ice removal, HVAC maintenance, carpet cleaning, and... miscellaneous.

When it comes to miscellaneous, mainly repairs, I'm at the mercy of chance. I just received a $350 bill for repairs to the rooftop HVAC discovered during routine maintenance. Unfortunately, not all repairs fall on the landlord. When the tech described the problem, he may as well repeated dialog from the Star Trek series and said, "The entire dilithium crystal converter assembly is fused." I honestly don't know what he said; I just wrote the check. What the FUTA?

Recounting her statement that she knows what the store makes, I say, "Do you really?" Looking at the bigger picture, after five years, I averaged selling over $250,000 worth of merchandise a year. A quarter of a million dollars! That sounds like a lot of money for a small business, or does it? Not so fast...

$250,000 minus $150,000 product cost minus $36,000 rent minus another $36,000 for payroll minus $891 insurance minus $4500 credit card processing fees minus $1050 HVAC necessary maintenance fees minus $600 security monitoring minus $3500 utilities minus $3000 advertising minus $2400 annual computer support minus $9773 state/federal social security matching and unemployment minus $1870 accounting fees minus $272 county personal property taxes leaves $144 for the year.

Consider the elusive miscellaneous charges, and you'll find yourself quickly in the red. There is some financial relief when products sell for more than the standard 40% earnings, as with the discontinued but highly sought-after items in the story mentioned prior. I make more when I work more of the hours. If we have mild weather, we save on utilities and could potentially have busier days. Still, she does not know what I make as a small business owner, not by a longshot.

As the taxes and bills increase
The debt and interest won't cease
With no end in sight
Can't give up the fight
With several more years on the lease

It was during one of these discouraging moments that I approached my landlord for a miracle fix. I asked him if he might or knew someone who might be interested in buying and taking over my store. Knowing what the bottom line would need to be, he quickly asked, "What are your annual gross register sales?" Trying to keep my shoulders from slumping, I replied, "just over $250,000." His face and his quick, blunt answer said it all, "I'll let you know if I do." He knew what I knew; the store was doing ok if the owner worked all or most of the hours.

I wasn't going to stop there and figured, "what the heck," and tried to turn the table in my favor by asking my landlord for reduced rent. As a naïve newbie to the retail world, I would soon find out that accountability comes with risk. The storefront chosen appeared to be adequate, even promising. It was newish, had some familiar names nearby, and a reasonably steady flow of cars. There were a few empty spots, but it began to hit home just how much better it would be if it were full. The thing is, I couldn't afford the rent in a packed and bustling location. My location could be moved into a busier section of the same complex and take the risk that extra foot traffic would outweigh increased rent, but did I want more risk? After struggling for the first few years, there was finally some profit coming in. I had my chip placed on a roulette wheel number and had no more control over neighbors as I did spinning that wheel.

I composed a beautifully written letter to my landlord, one that seemed wholly defensible and warranted. I suggested that he reduce my rent (red alert) just until additional neighbors signed on and foot traffic increased a bit. I respectfully asked for mercy while I struggled to keep my head afloat. Indeed, he would agree, right? Not long after he received my letter, I received an equally well-written letter with phrases like "we hear you" and "your words do not fall on deaf ears."

For some reason, this scenario seemed oddly familiar. I felt the lectures we delivered to our oldest son about "adulting" were now laughing and boomeranging. Unfortunately, it was now my turn to adult, and these teachings of small business ownership were not fun.

That's the difficulty of a small business; the smaller you are, the bigger your expenses are, in contrast. You'd think, small business, small space, equals small costs. But, unfortunately, the opposite is now true. Small companies are disadvantaged by technology; big companies are advantaged by it. Government agencies wallop small businesses; big businesses are privy to the loopholes.

When I first discussed essential matters with my accountant, he asked, "What kind of cost do you pay on the products you sell?" My reply was, "typically 50%," thinking that was good, and he quickly replied, "Let's hope it's a little better than that." That comment came well before the stores' first day and was my first clue that things might be a little more challenging than previously thought. It was the elephant in the room and was quickly brushed aside as I reassured myself by thinking, "He doesn't know what he's talking about." But he did.

What I didn't know was that he, too, had owned a small brick-and-mortar store. So, he not only knew the challenges that were coming my way, but he knew all too well the magnitude of expenses that would eat away at the other 50%. As the years ticked by, I would sarcastically ask him, "Do you want to buy a store?" He would inevitably throw his head back and roar in laughter. This guy had a larger-than-life personality, and his over-the-top belly laughs helped turn a sarcastic comment coming from a slightly injured ego into a much lighter feeling. Ok, he got it. At least someone does.

Like a hamster on a hamster wheel, I was mostly content. I wasn't going anywhere fast, but it was my decision to get on my wheel and how hard to run. Someday, hopefully, shoppers will tire of weaving through the masses of people while employees avoid eye contact and evasively duck down nearby aisles. Have you ever tried to find an employee to help you at a big box store? One can only hope for the eventual appreciation for the little guys who value their business. With this appreciation, the small business owner can justify the debt and the risk.

I end with a dialogue from a genuine customer. It begs the question, "Do I HAVE to pay for the entire purchase?" Yet, I did reign in a knee-jerk verbal reaction.

A priest, a rabbi, and a minister walk into the store. Just kidding! A woman walks into the store and selects four fragranced products. Her intended purchase includes the fragrance itself, one heavy lotion, one lighter lotion, and one shower gel, totaling just over $24.

Her: Can I have a break in the price since I'm buying four items?

Me: Our prices are pretty much at rock bottom already, I'm sorry, but I can't.

Her: She walks to the front door and LOUDLY hollers to her daughter, waiting in her car, "I need more money!"

Her: After gathering miscellaneous bills and change, dumping it, and counting it on the counter, and further realizing she still lacked the total amount, she announces to me, "I only have $22."

Me: Yes, the total is $24.

Her: Can I have one for free?

Me: You know, you have two varieties of the lotions; why don't you put one back, and then you'll have enough.

She did end up putting one of the lotions back, but really, can I have one for free?

My expectations were that EVERYONE understands the struggles of small businesses. We're surrounded by catchphrases supporting them. Thus, I expected complete understanding and support without question. Hardy har har.

In reality, though the majority of people feel for the little guy, many others mistakenly believe, "business owner equals rich person." And when it comes to government agencies, they don't seem to much care about the little guy. It's the opposite; loopholes are geared toward big business. The government agencies gifted the rest of us with tough love, "sink or swim baby, sink or swim."

Intermission

There was a store clerk who'd confess
Little knowledge of retail success
So sure she could run
And have lots of fun
A store but found out she was clueless

There were cheats and sneaks and thieves
An abundance of tricks up their sleeves
The deals weren't enough
They stole handfuls of stuff
And found numerous ways to deceive

Bending over backwards to accrue
Pleasant comments from a good review
Saying the wrong thing
Will certainly bring
A low rating and lost revenue

Shop small to support the little guy
As long as the prices are low, not high
A sale guarantee
Or better yet free
Or else they'll be saying goodbye

She jumped through the hoops that were there
Creating a store with some flair
But often was dazed
Her eyebrows were raised
In handling people with care

Taxes from city and county and fed
Assuring the store would stay in the red
A brick-and-mortar store
Turned quickly to a chore
Of credit debt and overhead

As the taxes and bills increase
The debt and interest won't cease
With no end in sight
Can't give up the fight
With several more years on the lease

Open the door to the public and grin
Lo and behold they begin to walk in
With children in tow
Mini tornado
Oblivious to chaos within

Finding a new perspective
Would help with over-reactive
Responses to those
Who tend to impose
Instead of being reflective

We now rely on computer support
Be wary of those who try to extort
Technology's no fun
From cards that won't run
And hoping that nothing falls short

The tears the laughs the lessons learned
The products bought and then returned
The skin that was thin
Is now like buckskin
A degree in resilience well-earned

Numbers begin to pull ahead
Could be our chance to get out of the red
But an epidemic
A crazy pandemic
Sets us back once again instead

"The Usual Suspects"

Chapter 10
The Good, The Bad, and The Bosses

Until owning a store, I'd only ever been an employee, never an employer or even a manager. My new adventure would teach me that there are perks to this boss thing, like turning over the demanding customers to fellow employees. However, all I knew from my 15 prior jobs, yes 15, was my desire to like my job well enough to not clock-watch. Beyond that, my hopes were for a pleasant boss, which I now strived to be.

The majority of my former jobs had one thing in common. They were mostly for relatively small companies, and I worked closely with my coworkers and the owners. Over the years, my bosses came in a strangely wide variety. I certainly had the work experience and job turnover to sample more than a few.

I rarely saw my first boss while working at a local public library. He was like the elusive Wizard of Oz; I knew he was behind his office door but rarely saw him. He existed, apparently, because he graced me with a nickel raise (woo-hoo) in the two years I worked there. My takeaway: you genuinely could manage people while at the same time avoiding them, I could relate to that.

Working in the food industry taught me this: I didn't want to work in the food industry. My boss was perched a few feet higher than the rest of us minions in a cage-like office; picture Louie DePalma on the TV show *Taxi*.

89

This boss let me know that my "boobs were too small to work the front register." Huh, interesting correlation. It set the bar extremely low; I could certainly do better than that one.

We all but forced our oldest son to work in food service to let him know what real work is. He was thrilled to start his new job, but his world collapsed after a mere one day on the job. He returned home and said, "I HATE that job!" My husband and I chuckled, thinking he was kidding. My son reiterated, "I'm serious; I HATE THAT JOB!" It turns out our son wasn't fond of scraping food plates with cigarette butts and wads of gum shoved into leftover half-chewed food. We both lost our smiles and instead went into teaching mode.

We insisted that he give the job a chance, and if, after six months, he still wants to quit, so be it. Our son was not pleased. He experienced what I would dub The Second Set of Parents at this job, as his boss(es) was a married couple. They took him under their wings and showed him the ropes, along with several audio presentations of how a couple interacts under pressure in a confined space. I'm confident the experience was good for him, but we had to laugh when he would often sum up his shifts with a grin and a simple "wow." After one notable work shift, he arrived home wearing "the look." He said, "I got to clean up an overflowed toilet tonight; that was a treat." He added that his boss handed him the cleaning supplies and said, "just take care of it." Any arrogance took a back seat that night. But, after being promoted to waiter, things fell into a more positive light. Humility can be a good thing, and it's essential to be at both ends of the spectrum. Long story short, after his first hissy fit, he went back to work, for seven years, through high school and college. He ended up loving the job.

I once worked for Dr. Jekyll and Mr. Hyde; I could've done without that one. One unforgettable day (there were many), a woman called and described a terrifying man to me. She cried, and her voice shook throughout the description. She said he was in the company vehicle and she'd like to talk to my boss about him, to which I replied: "That IS the boss." The funny thing was, my first impression of him during my interview was, "definitely the nicest guy in the world." Wrong! Ever since that out-of-whack first impression, I've questioned my judgement.

The Social Butterfly Boss was actually several bosses I had while working at a discount merchandise store. They were far more interested in socializing (really socializing) than they were in managing the store. I watched with amazement as a gaggle of young managers and their subordinates acted more like college frat boys and sorority sisters, breaking up not one but two of their marriages and almost a third. As a sixteen-year-old, it was an eyeful as I watched their unfortunate spouses filing in, trying to look run-of-the-mill while spying on their not-so-better halves. It was tragic, but interesting, and I was again learning what NOT to do.

I've had incredibly unethical bosses and others that could've taught ethics classes. Some had extreme tempers that, to this day, provided amusing stories but weren't so funny at the time. A couple of bosses were father figures to me after losing my own at age 19, while others were very withdrawn and distant. It's truly astonishing how different they were from one another. So I shouldn't have been surprised when finding myself in their position but feeling a bit lost as I stepped out of my comfort zone.

My comfort zone was a career that enabled me to keep to myself. It began with a high school drafting course and ultimately college classes that centered largely around subdivision design. I comfortably sat behind a drafting table, by myself, and ultimately behind a computer screen, by myself. It was a far cry from selling beauty products to, OMG, people.

My tendencies toward detail and precision, or as my first boss in the field called it, "square to the world," was an asset in both drafting and store ownership. So, when times changed and the art form of drafting morphed with the computer age, I didn't adapt well and began to clock-watch. Not only was I doing the minimum expected of me, but I began to despise the work.

Towards the tail end of my computer career I had a female boss, a civil engineer, who was as gracious as she was giving, the exact opposite of female superiors I'd had in the past. She had hired me years before, when I was visibly pregnant, speaking volumes by that action alone.

Several years into my job, she approached me and gently told me that my heart didn't seem to be in my work anymore; she was correct. But instead of firing me, which I likely deserved, she let it go with the subtle suggestion. At that point, I was there merely for the money and the flexibility she offered; I was taking advantage of her good nature. She could probably relate to the difficulties I would face years later when adopting a similar approach of subtle suggestions.

The decision was made to take my part-time hobby of selling beauty products full-time into a brick-and-mortar setting. Not much thought was given to my subsequent need for employees and the relationship shared with them. I had personally experienced a motley assortment of employers. They had techniques varying from distant, bordering on reclusive, to respectable and professional, to unfortunately, overbearing and shocking. Their personalities and problem-solving skills were equally as intriguing…

I worked my tail off writing legal descriptions for hundreds of properties at one engineering/surveying firm. Finally, after proudly announcing to my boss that I had finished in several weeks what he thought would take several months, steam came out of his ears. Barely containing his percolating anger (he was p*ssed off), he made his point clear by stating, "You're working yourself out of a job." That was a weird lesson in (air quotes, please), "pacing myself."

This job was directly followed by quite the opposite and a very different employer, for whom I couldn't work fast enough. The numerous but small drawings were pumped out in a half-hours time each. At $12 an hour, I received $6 for each drawing, to which he took a quick (uh, very quick) look, then signed off and charged the client $110. That became a lesson in not only the value of a signature from a licensed professional but, more importantly, keeping your employees on task. When I slacked off and began taking 45 minutes per drawing, my boss swiftly sat me down in his office. He explained that the drawings NEED to get out in a half-hours time, not 45 minutes. He wasn't mean, just authoritative, and although a bit miffed, I knew my place. There was no doubt about it; this guy maximized his profits.

My introverted personality would be a stumbling block. I couldn't see myself sitting anyone down for a "little talk." I was amused when my husband described a former employer of his. This guy's approach to problem-solving was handling a situation while completely avoiding it. I could identify with this guy; he was a perfect example of a passive-aggressive boss...

The shoe store treatment was what my husband coined the finale of a job he held more than 30 years ago at the tail end of his college years. He worked at a shoe store that had a policy stating, "If a woman comes in looking for a particular pair of shoes, present those shoes and a pair of the exact opposite." So, if the woman asked for a pair of pumps, he presented them along with a pair of tennis shoes. Then, in an attempt to further upsell her purchase, he was to suggest a matching handbag. But, he explains, "I was never a convincing enough salesman to do either of those things. Though I feel I was an excellent shoe salesman, selling multiple pairs or matching handbags wasn't going to happen." The consequences were dire but funny. After about two months on the job, he goes in to check his schedule and asks the boss what hours he will be working the following week. The boss replies, "Uh, yeah, you're not working any hours next week." My husband responds, "What about the next week?" His boss replies, "Uh, you're not working that week, either." Finally, he got the point that he was being let go, but he added, "Technically, I still work there."

My expectations were that I would do it my way, including accommodating my comfort zone. My wish was to run a store, not be a boss, or worse yet, be bossy.

In reality, I would at no point give anyone the shoe store treatment, but I WAS passive-aggressive, and that can cause problems. But, all in all, my employees were what I needed to provide a mixture of personalities and bring balance to working with the public.

*"Problematic Customer?
Gosh, would you look at the time?!"*

Chapter 11
Sharing the Load

So, it was my turn to try a hand at this boss thing. It was one more matter that I figured out (sort of) as I went along. I would end up with far more good experiences than not and have been pleasantly surprised on many occasions. My employees genuinely cared about the store and certainly had more patience than I with customers, way more. There were times that a problematic customer would come in, and I'd sheepishly smile at my employee before bolting out of the room to let them deal with it.

I've had employees go out of their way with ideas on doing things better, even dipping into their own money to buy supplies to furnish their ideas. And I was thrilled to find an online comment on one gal who was working her tail off when I wasn't there. She also knew how to upsell products, something I never had the boldness to do, but the sales from her shifts reflected her efforts.

Since I was no longer alone in my work, my job duties suddenly shifted from doing everything myself to delegating things to others. Delegating was never and will never be my strong suit. I'm not comfortable with it and would often say one thing but expect another. For instance, I highly encouraged a laid-back work environment, including a backdrop of ones' favorite movie or Netflix TV show on the store's flatscreen TV. Though customers took priority, rest breaks were encouraged "whenever." At the same time, I expected a frenzied, almost frantic work pace. There were a lot of mixed messages coming out of my mouth. But in all fairness, by and large, my employees worked diligently on their merit and needed no instruction. Additionally, they sometimes gave me suggestions to find a necessary backbone at times.

In revisiting my own personal work history, I was generally a good employee over the years. However, I'd often clock-watch and remember once falling asleep on my drafting table long enough to leave a drool spot on my drawing, literally. Now that the tables were turned, I had to realize that people are human, including myself. So, I largely learned by reviewing my own personality and contradictions.

One winter day, I came into the store and seen an unusual amount of salt had been tracked in. It was scattered on the entry tile and carpet and trailed onto the main area. There was A LOT, and it looked as if no one had vacuumed for quite some time. I said, "Wow, look at all this salt!" hoping my hint was more than just a hint. Unfortunately, my indirect statement yielded nothing except to leave the cleanup for myself later that day. I could have said, "Do you mind vacuuming this salt? It's getting kind of bad." That request wouldn't have been out of line at all, but a timid nature was so ingrained in me; I couldn't find it in myself to verbalize anything that sounded like an order. The blame was mine; I couldn't expect everyone to read my mind.

In wanting to be generous with pay and raises, I jumped the gun and handed them out based on wishful thinking. I incorrectly assumed the growth witnessed in years two and three would continue. Instead of waiting for the store's challenges to level out, I paid more than 50% higher than the minimum wage from the get-go. Additionally, raises weren't based on merit but rather at regular intervals to everyone. I had a reckless government spending attitude. The problem was, I wasn't raiding the taxpayers' pot of money, it was my own.

And it wasn't so much that the wages paid were extravagantly high, but more in that my store wasn't pulling in the money needed to support even modestly higher wages; few do. After selecting the location for the store, I assumed that more stores/neighbors would soon follow, filling the empty sites as my numbers soared. I overlooked the obvious, what if the vacant sites don't fill? They didn't, and I found myself amidst mediocre foot traffic and fierce competition with the larger stores, growing internet sales, and home delivery.

I was kept on my toes, trying to stay one step ahead of a partially full strip mall's snowball effect. There have been days when the sole employee didn't drive themselves to work but rather, are driven to the store by a friend or family member. Without a car parked directly in front, my store space now looks like the vacant spaces nearby and could potentially lose considerable income that day.

There was a fine line, and I found myself walking a tightrope. At that moment, although payroll was tight, I was sitting pretty comfortably with employees who could work solo and were trustworthy. Reality would be put into perspective for me one evening with a phone call from another dimension...

An applicant, so to speak, made me appreciate the employees I had and let me know that I was sitting pretty. This lesson is two-fold. One, there are consequences to putting your cell phone number out there. Two, never, ever answer the phone during the season finale of your favorite TV show. On this particular evening, I was excited, REALLY excited, as I found myself minutes away from the season finale of "The Walking Dead."

My bowl of popcorn was sitting by the couch when my phone rang. At the same time, my inner voice was screaming at me not to answer it. I've never been one to screen calls or force people to leave messages, so I reluctantly answered it. The voice on the other end was either on drugs or extremely intoxicated and found it funny to ask for a job while screaming profanities and busting out laughing. I actually had to hold the phone away from my head; it was that loud and obnoxious. But of course, living in this insane world of political correctness, I responded politely (which almost seemed foolish), only to be forced to hold the phone away again with another attack. Finally, when it became glaringly apparent that the call was going nowhere, I hung up.

Of course, it rang again, and whatever obsession I have with answering the phone made me pick it up for another onslaught, but even angrier and peppered with the B word. As much as I loathe technology, my "block this caller" function came in handy that day. Long story short, the prologue to my show was ruined with this ridiculous call. But, this lovely applicant abruptly put any petty concerns about employees or pay into perspective.

Riding the wave with a wait-and-see approach seemed to be the correct course of action. I felt pretty good about myself when the stars aligned, and the flow of business was steady. During those times, sales would fund payroll and then some, and there would be the ideal amount of time to clean and put out merchandise. On the other hand, I felt equally miserable when the weather turned ever so slightly or I lost a neighboring business and their foot traffic. Almost every time I felt good about myself and the store, reality gave me a swift kick through issues beyond my control. The truth was, there were many factors besides what I was paying for an hourly wage; it was the whole ball of wax.

An online quote by D. Ridgley summarized why a little humility might be in order. He said, "Listening to others' viewpoints may reveal the one thing needed to complete your goals." And that's where the balance was; I wasn't alone and there were many times I needed the respite. I also had to swallow my pride when realizing that sometimes my employees could see things I could not.

In planning my first and upcoming store inventory, I devised a plan to count and record everything. To put it mildly, it was a cumbersome plan. One of my employees suggested a completely different approach, and although my ego found it painful, she was right. Her method ended up being a huge time saver.

Another time a different employee suggested reducing the number of store coupons that were handed out like candy. Considerable money was walking out the door for not a lot of return. I thought it was a nice gesture, but as my employee politely pointed out, it was unnecessary and even foolish on my part. She, too, saved me money and helped me get a backbone in becoming a little more responsible.

For being in the business of selling primarily beauty products, I use very little makeup. I'm what you might call low maintenance. On the flip side, most of my employees were all-girl, and it helped to have them there to fill in when I struggled. And then of course, my younger gals did what younger people do, technology. When it came to social media, I often said with some embarrassment, "Can you help me figure this out?"

What one employee lacked, another excelled at, and vice-versa; they all indeed did have something to offer. Management was a challenge for me, and I beat myself up far too often about it. But, like so many other areas of store ownership, I was forced to look inward and learned more about myself than any potential problem.

My expectations regarding employees were, "What's for dinner?" There wasn't much thought because I didn't believe there'd be anything to think about.

In reality, passive-aggressive is my middle name, and I lived and died by the rule, "avoid anything you're not comfortable with, just in case." Any problems existed because of my lazy safe place and my quick impulse to lay blame where it probably didn't belong. With time, I came to own it.

"Unattended children will receive a double caffeine latte and a puppy upon their departure"

Chapter 12
Puppies, Lattes, and Sneaky Pete

On the front window of the store, next to the front door, hung a sign that read, "Unattended children will receive a double caffeine latte and a puppy upon their departure." I wish I could take credit for the clever wording, but I saw it hanging at a local thrift store and stole the idea. Nevertheless, it hung there, amusing many shoppers but largely ignored by the ones it targets.

Long before opening day, I imagined what the store would look like and what my customers might be like. I naively expected a bunch of average Joes and Janes. More specifically, I expected GROWN UP Joes and Janes; I didn't think about their smaller versions. My fellow employees helped in sharing the occasional burden and subsequent cleanup, and the stories.

Open the door to the public and grin
Lo and behold they begin to walk in
With children in tow
Mini tornado
Oblivious to chaos within

There were quite a few makeup testers that fell victim to the lightning-fast skills of a toddler. The only good thing was that the testers were frequently replaced and refreshed because of it, but that cost money. My smallest customers would weeble-wobble along the display shelves, unattended, practicing their "doink doink boop boop" skills. Mom, auntie, or grandma lingered a mere five to ten feet away, minding their own business, while this scenario repeated itself on a semi-regular basis.

One memorable day a mother, a grandmother, and their two-year-old little girl walk in. The grandmother immediately hooks a leash up to the two-year-old, to which I think to myself, "Good; maybe they'll keep her under control." Wrong! After approximately one to two minutes, grandma lets go of the leash, and little Suzie snowflake runs amuck. She grabs two available teddy bears (new ones for sale, not meant to be schlepped around on the floor), one in each hand, and continues her path of destruction. Mom completely ignores her while grandma occasionally glances in her direction while, with a meaningless sideways comment, utters, "no, stop that."

She topples over items that are (were) neatly displayed, many of which domino due to their awkward packaging. Anything from the ground up to a three-foot height is fair game. Snowflake heads over to the boxed lipsticks and begins to tear them open, to which I dart over, guiding her hands away while telling mom, "If these seals get opened, we can't sell them." Her response was, "Oh, she's such a busy little girl; she's like this at home too." She then smiles and continues shopping. Oh, well, ok then. Sweating profusely, I pop in a children's movie and hand snowflake a children's book, hoping to divert her attention, and save my store. Mom and grandma continue about their business while I, the shop owner, try to entertain the child (however cute) dragging the useless leash behind her, who prefers toppling products to any child's book or movie—finally, the threesome leave. Products are strewn about on the floor, and upon their departure, mom remarks, literally, "I'm sorry we destroyed your store," to which I smile. Forever at the mercy of social media, the customer IS always right.

Although unruly children have come and gone, one other will forever stand out in my mind that I shared a long-overdue conversation. This little guy, age three or four, comes in with grandma. Grandma couldn't care less what he was doing. It was highly likely that it was a pleasure for her to put him in someone else's hands for half an hour while she enjoyed some time to herself. He beelined to a seating area I had towards the back of the store, consisting of two leather chairs and an ottoman.

A cross between a gymnast and a wildcat, he begins jumping from one chair to the ottoman to the other chair and back. He does it repeatedly, back and forth, over and over. It seemed like an eternity of watching the springs in my furniture scream as carefree grandma continued to shop as if nothing was wrong, just ten feet away.

Besides the potential damage, as well as the lack of respect for someone else's property, I sensed a lawsuit around the corner if this kid fell into a multitude of potential objects. I walked over and strategically timed a little talk to the child when grandma was out of earshot. My narrowed (stink) eyes zeroed in on him as I lowered myself onto the ottoman. He paused long enough to make eye contact while I summoned my evil twin. In a subdued voice, I said, "This is my furniture, and you have no right to jump on my furniture." After one more "look," as only a woman can do, he slid back into the chair. Though he looked puzzled with this new concept of behaving appropriately, he also looked angelic for the time being. While I was performing an exorcism on myself, grandma took notice of this strange behavior. She said, "What did you say to him? He never listens to me." to which my good twin replied and said, "Oh, not much," followed by a smile.

Unquestionably some adults act like children in wanting me to explain the unexplainable regarding discontinued products and price hikes. I often took liberties in creative wording. I got so good at it, I almost scared myself.

"Why do they discontinue my stuff?" It's one of those sentences that when I hear the first three words, "why do they," my teeth clench, and the veins pop out of my neck. One woman was looking for a discontinued face cream, and opens her own, very old bottle of cream, complete with a thick yellow crust on the rim. She bought it years ago and is just now back to replenish. Putting aside the fact she still put that on her face, I had to answer the age-old question... why do they discontinue the stuff you rarely use? Hmmm, I'll answer that in a minute... Another woman walks in with a dated crème blush stick. She even admitted that it was, in her words, "really old." We happened to make the same product; however, it'd been repackaged into a container half the original size. This one product was indeed a pox upon me as I found myself trying to explain over and over that yes, sometimes products are resized smaller, AND the price goes up. She gasped at the fact that it was half the size and double the cost. She'd now have to replace this $7 product once every year or two instead of three or four. She added that the color didn't look the same, no doubt from years of contamination by skin oils, makeup and bacteria. Other times there is no suitable replacement, and they leave, but not before a slightly snippy verbal reprimand of "I guess I'll just have to shop somewhere else." OH SNAP!

There's a good number of reasons that affect a product's availability, none of which the store owner can control. The companies certainly can't be TRYING to upset customers. I've heard that key ingredients frequently either become unavailable or become too costly to continue using. Sometimes they become prohibited for one reason or another (scary). More often it's a matter of making room for new trends. Regardless, I'm the bearer of the bad news and in anticipation of the blowback I try to begin my ramble with calming words: "Well, these things can be complicated." Once I slipped up with frankness and said, "Companies sometimes need to make room for new products." That was a huge mistake as the customer spit nails and let me have it, "I don't want new products; I want my old product!!!" Over the years, finding what to say and what not to say was my saving grace; and less was usually better. More often than not, I'll scrunch my face and say, "I'm so sorry," and hope my apology with a little scratching behind their ears is ample.

"Sneaky Pete" embodied adult problem behavior. Kids sometimes lie or steal, but when adults do it, it can cause some real harm. Sneaky Pete charges over $100 and runs a credit card that is promptly declined. Sneaky says, "Just a second, I'll be right back," then walks out to the parking lot and out of view, returning a few minutes later carrying a cell phone playing a recorded message that says, "A charge for $100.xx has been applied to your card from such and such store." Sneaky stares on while I scratch my head, assuming that I'll blindly accept the message and hand over the product. Sneaky doesn't know that the legal banking name, the one that would be in a genuine message, isn't the name on the front of the store. Holding my ground that day, I was caught off balance

110

and questioned what was happening, but I did hold my ground. I usually go on the adage that the customer is right and rarely risk accusing them for fear of making a mistake. But nothing felt right about the situation.

Other customers (most of them, really) create a joyful balance. One customer was VERY enthusiastic and spread the word about my store to her friends and family. She is the ideal customer. One day, she came bounding in with a friend in tow. The friend was equally excited because of the excitement surrounding her friend. They spent a half-hour shopping, talking, and laughing while filling their baskets. I watched from behind the counter while trying to contain myself, "Don't act too excited, don't act too excited!" It was the moment once described by an online meme that said, "When you buy from a small business, an actual person does a little happy dance." When they made their purchases, they each spent close to $200, and I was elated. They then apologized for being loud, to which I quickly let them know there was no need to apologize. I added, "Do you know that your purchase is the same amount that I'll make for an entire day on some days?" It was indeed cause for a happy dance.

My expectations were that I'd have short interactions with customers in a small store, but in reality, you have in-depth and fascinating ones. To a certain point, you get to know them, for better or for worse.

"At closing time Mrs. Smith arrives…for an hour"

Chapter 13
Finding a New Perspective

Unrealistic expectations can happen on both sides of the aisle, for both customers and store employees. For instance, if closing time is 7:00, and a customer walks in at 6:55, they have every right to do so. But, there's a big HOWEVER in that statement, and it involves about 5 to 10 minutes, maybe 15. Simple annoyances and unique personalities needed a new perspective, and that was frequently humor...

Mrs. Smith came in on a semi-regular basis, always at closing time and always intending to stay awhile. She took it upon herself to dub herself, "After Hours Alice," which was amusingly ironic considering her habit wasn't exactly a good habit. In the beginning, every customer received the benefit of the doubt. We followed questionable behavior with comments like, "Oh, don't worry about it!" or "It's no problem!" Over time, I'm not sure if I became a schmuck, or family.

Soon after arriving precisely at closing time, after the front door was locked and the first bank of lights were turned off, Alice would predictably and comfortably take a seat with every intention on staying awhile. In one case, I clearly had somewhere to be and bluntly stated that I needed to be there within the hour. She not only didn't acknowledge my announcement, and yes, she could hear just fine, but it didn't seem to concern her one way or the other. So, much like family, she went about her business with friendly small talk while discussing her likes and dislikes about every product past and present. Privy to information about her upcoming surgeries, past surgeries, family news, and the status of the world made for some lengthy conversations. The more I fretted and sweated, the more she found to talk about.

I barely made it to my prior engagement on time, but only after changing pleasant dinner plans to a less desirable but much speedier restaurant. It wasn't unusual for Alice to stay for close to an hour after closing the store.

She got a little too comfortable when she phoned another evening and spoke with one of my employees very near closing time. After announcing that she was on her way, she added that "we'd better be there." We took the good with the bad as she typically made respectably sized purchases, and she was nice, even entertaining. As time went on, she added an increasingly high return rate to her after-hour visits as we shrugged, smiled and rolled our eyes; after all, it's ok, it's just Alice. I guess she really did become more and more like family as boundaries fell by the wayside.

Finding a new perspective
Would help with over-reactive
Responses to those
Who tend to impose
Instead of being reflective

Mrs. Smith was one of many that, putting their intriguing habits aside, were very likable people. It's hard to be too mad at them, even when they push the envelope. I look back with fondness, and on some weird level I will miss her…and the others.

One of the others was a customer who showed up with her very large dog. After asking permission, which I granted with confidence (what could go wrong?), she strolled over to the register area where the dog promptly took a lengthy squat. Large dogs make large messes; that carpet was soaked. I stared on but remained silent while she had that, "move along, nothing to see here" approach to the situation. The cleanup was left for me while pondering the question, "what's the deal?" Fortunately, it was a one-time occurrence, and moreover, I'm a fan of dogs, and of course, paying customers.

It's been fun to be a spectator of sorts, standing on one side of the counter while observing the captivating habits of those on the other side. Sometimes I'd catch myself in a trance, robotically performing my duties, while staring at something interesting. You know how a dog or cat stares at you, but then will break from its own gaze to chew on their tail or lick their leg? Well, I did watch, everything, while still performing my normal day-to-day duties and it was endlessly fascinating. I no longer had the need or desire to clock-watch with this ever-changing scenery. Time flew by in this spectator sport.

Jane Wallet was one of those eye-catching customers. Jane carried a wallet much like the "exploding wallet" on the TV show Seinfeld. When she was ready for her purchase, my eyes widened and my vigilance would ramp up as Jane opened the precarious wallet. She would catch and retrieve falling receipts like snowflakes falling, ones that were apparently trying to come up for air after being smothered. Then, credit card roulette would begin within a mini rolodex file in her wallet, containing a multitude of bank cards in varying stages of decomposition. Several card contenders were selected and then held like a handful of playing cards while the decision was made of which one yet had ten or twenty dollars remaining.

I braced myself while sliding the card of choice, fully expecting a declined message, but Jane possessed powers that defied ordinary. She knew those cards; she memorized card numbers, balances, and due dates. I felt a little guilty, like a dealer in Vegas that just knew this player really shouldn't be at the table any longer. But I didn't know her story or her finances, and it wasn't up to me to question it.

Jane Wallet and Mrs. Smith gave me insight into other worlds that would have remained hidden while working in my cubicle jobs. Distancing myself from my old, insulated desk and its' five-foot walls taught me that I was sometimes wrong about my quick judgments, and that there's a whole 'nother world ripe for exploring. People are generally likeable despite our differences.

"There is nothing noble to being
superior to your fellow men.
True nobility lies in being
superior to your former self."
- Ernest Hemingway

The following narrative falls squarely in my court. There were several times I received a wake-up call as to my behavior, and this was one of them. To keep me from remaining in a permanent cringe-state, I must humbly accept my flaws. In working with customers whose paths crossed mine sometimes once, sometime only a handful of times, there really weren't any consequences to brutal honesty on their part. Because of this, my flaws were pointed out on occasion...

I fully admit that I have no gift for remembering names, faces, and details, which can be a real problem. Recalling my bosses' words at an old job drives home not only how poor my memory can be, but that it's no secret; he reminded me in a non-nonsense way. When a coworker asked me for more information on a job site we worked on the previous day, my boss couldn't chime in quick enough. He hollered from across the very small work space, "What the F*$K are you asking her for? She can't f*$king remember what she had for lunch today." Although I believe he was fond enough of me (yes, I'm serious), he didn't mince words, not at all. Plus, he liked to use the F word, a lot.

117

Fast forward to a day at the store when my curse reared its head high after hearing some very cringe-worthy words. On this day, my attempt at trying to be a warm and welcoming store owner backfired. My brain, in particular the section for memory, was only partially functioning, as usual. A female customer was browsing the store, making light conversation during which she mentioned her profession as a home health care nurse visiting from another state. She alternates spending two weeks here then returns home for the other two weeks, some five or six hours away. Finding this fascinating, I raised my eyebrows and genuinely said with some excitement, "OH REALLY?!" She gave me the "You're truly are a moron" look, and then she said, "Yeah, and we go through this EVERY TIME I'M HERE."

I stood frozen for a second, processing a reply in which there is no good reply, shrunk several inches, and smiled one doofus of a smile as my tail curled in-between my legs. After delivering my weak apology and repeating to myself, "For crying out loud, remember her face, remember her face!" I murmured a reply. My pathetic response was, "Well, I guess I'll remember you now." Boy, I hope I remember her next time. I take that back, if there's one face that's burned into my mind, it's hers.

My years of alone time in previous jobs haunt me occasionally with periods of selfishness; sometimes, I want to be left alone. During slow periods at the store, I'll drift into "me time" and take it a step too far in

118

wanting all "me time." Shocking as it sounds, when I'm in one of my moods, I'll actually get annoyed when I hear a customer walk through the door. It's a bad attitude when you're in sales, even if you are feeling standoffish.

One slow day I was immersed in computer work when a customer walked in, to which I mumbled, "dammit." After walking to the sales floor, I proceeded with tending to her needs in a pleasant but mostly all business manner.

During the sale, I noted my lousy attitude and, even more so, her demeanor. She seemed quiet and a bit lonely. I felt of rush of shame and mentally told myself to change my attitude and be quick about it. She made a conscious effort to choose to shop at my store; the least I could do was reciprocate with undivided attention. Instead of rushing the rest of the transaction, I slowed down and started some chit-chat. She perked up when the conversation steered toward her favorite country singer and a concert she recently attended. I was only mildly familiar with the artist she spoke of but leaned over and searched him up on the computer.

After playing a partial u-tube video of him and letting her finish her story of meeting him, she was visibly delighted to have been given the time to share her story and be heard. Then, she went on her way but not before telling me, "You just made my day!" It struck me like a slap in the face, one that I sorely needed, just how easy it was and how little time it took to make a difference in someone's happiness and, in turn, mine as well. Something as small as being mentally present for this customer made a genuine, positive difference.

One of my favorite authors, Wayne Dyer, said, "If you change the way you look at things, the things you look at change." Thankfully, I began to change how I looked at things and had the great fortune of a unique experience.

As a small business, there were frequently only one or two customers shopping at a time. This presented an optimal setting to talk to customers, sometimes at great length. There typically was no line of people waiting and no need to rush transactions. My seating area was used on several occasions for close conversation, almost as a small therapy corner. On one occasion, I casually took a seat with a customer who needed someone to talk to; we spoke for close to an hour without interruption. I knew better than to offer much advice, but I did lend an ear.

As a sidenote, I also learned that for a small business, generally staffed by one person, there is no quicker way to get a customer in the door than preparing lunch and casually sitting down to eat it. It's one of the rules of the universe. I would often put in a movie, and then circle the comfy chair and footrest like a lion waiting for its meal while my food warmed in the microwave. The ding of the microwave and the ding from the front door were predictably and practically simultaneous most every time. My customers would often kindly remark, "oh no, you were trying to eat your meal! Just relax, I'll shop, pretend I'm not here." Ok, they were nice about it, really nice.

My expectations for dealing with customers were all business. I thought there would be minimal and trifling conversations with them because I didn't know they would want much more from me.

The reality was very different. Some people enjoy a much more intimate setting and warm up to the store owner and staff quickly. One of my regulars literally told me, "I come here when I'm depressed, and it makes me feel better." WHOA! That was almost validation overload. It was like she took my face in her hands as she told me those words. Some people liked to talk, and others needed to talk. It wasn't all business; in reality, although fleeting, it was unexpected friendships.

"POS, point of sale? I can think of a more appropriate acronym…"

Chapter 14
That P.O.S.

While trying to master your people skills, you're simultaneously trying to grasp technology and its' ever-changing nature. To the rescue come the larger businesses who send minions into the much smaller ones offering services that will help (wink wink nod nod). The thing is, you don't have much choice. You'll pay, or "you'll pay."

Without computer support, if my sole computerized register breaks down in the middle of the day, I can't fix it. It teeters on extortion to have a team of IT people on hand and paid-up front. I say extortion because, apples to apples, a large corporation pays pennies on the dollar compared to what the little guys do. When it comes to advertising and internet search engines, if I don't pay to get my name out there, it disappears along with any descriptive information on how to find me. It's impossible for a small business that buys on a smaller scale to compete with corporations that get everything bulk rate.

When I was 16 years old, my job at a store similar to a modern-day Walmart or Target included cashier work. In those days (1983), we used a basic cash register, which I now see as a thing of beauty. You didn't have to program it, you didn't have to pay someone to set it up, and you weren't at the mercy of inconceivable problems only solvable by a computer support team.

To set up my modest 1600 s.f. retail store, I needed a point-of-sale system, a.k.a., POS. As a sidenote, there are much more colorful words for THAT acronym. I toggled with the idea of regressing and using price stickers and a traditional cash register, but the influence from peer pressure (other small business owners) convinced me otherwise. They said, "If you want to take your business seriously, you need a POS. Unfortunately, that one POS system was expensive, and I was to find out that it was only the beginning. Having a small business doesn't work to your advantage when furnishing it, essentially the same as a big box store, but lacks corporate volume buying power benefits.

After my check cleared, the company that sold me my POS sent out a guru to set it up and sit with me on my first two days to make sure I understood the basics. Albeit reassuring to have her with me those two days, the pressure was on for me to pay close attention to understand this thorny piece of equipment. It was a lot of responsibility, and for the first time in my life, there was no one in the next cubicle to run to for any questions coming my way. However, I did make it clear that she created a POS that was as idiot-proof as possible. I wanted a screen that looked like it was geared for a second-grader. I didn't want options or multiple screens. If I didn't need it, I didn't want to see it.

Over time I found that it was still WAY more machine than the store needed. It was also problematic for a new store because there weren't many customers coming through the door those first two days. I had only a few opportunities to run actual purchases through my new cash register while help was standing right next to me.

Even in creating a POS system that was by and large, simplistic, there were still problems coming my way. Unless you hire IT people to run your register, there will be confusion and mistakes. I once arrived to find a stack of receipts next to the cash register. The pile included voids, some returns that didn't look quite right, and some canceled sales. My employee remarked, "Oh, I need to show you those," and then thumbed through them, saying things like, "This is…well, wait, no, this one is, no, oh hell, I can't remember!" I'm left standing there a bit panicky; how much damage had been done in the past few hours? Secondly, if there was damage done, was it in my favor or the customers' favor? Because I'd always prefer a mistake to be in the customers' favor. An angry customer can only mean one thing, a future scowl followed by the question, "are you the owner?"

The new and improved cash register is a very complicated, extremely needy computer system with a maze of computer units, wires, and software, all of which are monitored remotely by a point-of-sale computer support team. They raided my newly created small business account for $10,000 to set up my single cash register and begin my computer support. It didn't end there.

Every August after that, I opened my yearly $2400 bill to renew my contract for computer support, and for that, they would be there, just in case. Just in case of what you ask? Just in case the damn thing decides to break down, which it does on a semi-regular basis. I often question if it's programmed with a FAIL program that goes off intermittently. This way, a call is made to have them rescue me, to which I say, "Thank goodness I have computer support; that's worth every penny!"

One such day my employee called and informed me that she couldn't run credit cards. Those are scary words; most customers no longer carry ANY cash. The screen displayed an error message saying, "term not active, 402, not approved." It could have said "need software update," but then I might not need a computer support team. To figure out the actual meaning of "term not active, 402, not approved" took quite a few phone calls, swearing, a headache, and of course, another bill.

We now rely on computer support
Be wary of those who try to extort
Technology's no fun
From cards that won't run
And hoping that nothing falls short

My computer support team informed me that my machine needed a software update and I was promptly emailed a sales order agreement. This agreement stated that they would upgrade the software for $185, to which I replied, "What?!" Somewhere in the small print of our original agreement, it states that the support for which I pay $2400/year doesn't cover software upgrades or even the monitoring of the upgrades. That's found out when we process a sale and am greeted with an error message centered perfectly in the middle of the dreaded blank screen. For extra fun, it's encrypted, or may as well be.

Reluctantly the sales order agreement was signed, and I say reluctantly, as the entire second and third page of said sales order agreement included 15 paragraphs of mind-boggling legal phrases. This purposely confusing language had, "Distributor's obligations hereunder shall be limited solely to distributor making." What? I think this one was clear, "Customer hereby waives any claim customer may have against distributor." My takeaway from that is that it's most definitely NOT in my favor. The confusion continued with, "Customer further agrees that distributor will not be liable, regardless of the form of action, whether in contract or in tort including negligence," meaning they can do whatever they want.

My rights were all but given up. And using words like "tort," seemed, ridiculous. Next, they added "Solely and entirely customer's responsibility," which didn't sound good. The grand finale was in big, bold letters spelling out, "CUSTOMER ACKNOWLEDGES THAT IT HAS READ THIS AGREEMENT, AND UNDERSTANDS AND AGREES TO ALL TERMS AND CONDITIONS STATED HEREIN."

I understand that the sole purpose of the agreement, written by corrupt lawyers, is to take away all my rights. Additionally, I'm a little fearful of a future conversation containing the phrase, "You should have known better."

Shortly after that fiasco, a well-intentioned but disappointed customer asked, "Don't you have a chip reader for credit cards yet?" It blew the wind out of my sails. I felt like some little kid running a Kool-Aid stand with my change bucket when I replied, "no, I don't have a chip reader." Who would've thought there would be a "keep up with the Joneses" mentality in retail equipment options? Frozen with fear and picturing not only the software upgrades but the accompanying hardware, my mind spins, fretting, "Now how much will THAT cost me?" And yes, my now eight-year-old system, ancient by tech standards, will probably be incompatible with the new hardware. It felt like I was playing Monopoly, and I just landed on my opponents Boardwalk space, with two hotels on it, and they were smirking at me. How much is the computer upgrade?!

After calling my computer support team, they warned me that credit card companies have recently made it easier for users to dispute (and erase) charges on their cards with one all-too-easy click of a button. As human nature would have it, some people took advantage of this new option meant with good intentions, but were now abusing it. The store owner is then out the money unless THEY decide to fight it, a time-consuming process.

I've never had the unfortunate experience of a disputed charge, as I've been fortunate that my clientele is, by and large, honest. Nevertheless, it's one more item clogging up the "If this happens, you'll need to do this" section of my brain. Unless the fraudulent charge is sizeable, chances are the owner will not proceed with a formal dispute.

My expectations regarding technology were that I would rarely have to deal with it when running a small business. It's one of the main reasons I left my career of 25 years; the transition to computers all but forced me to go.

In reality, you can rarely escape technology in the workplace. "Technology makes it possible for people to gain control over everything, except over technology."
– John Tudor

"@#$%!...I mean, Can I help you?"

Chapter 15
An Against You Kind of Day

I'm not a fan of technology; that's obvious. Technology and my bad view towards it came to bite me the day I discovered a problem with the work computer. Finding this information was only a tiny part of an exhausting day.

On this particular day, I should have just called in sick but realistically couldn't. I came in with a bad attitude and I didn't want to be there. The universe's rules then summoned the predictable lineup of demanding customers in tandem with a string of challenges joining forces to break my temperament, as it often did. If you work in a cubicle, you can typically get away with a day like this by slumping in your chair and avoiding most, if not all, human contact. In a store, it's far more problematic. If you've ever read the book "The Secret," you know your attitude can work for you or against you. I will describe an against you kind of day.

My fragile day began with, "Stay calm, and this too will pass, all 9 1/2 hours of it." The store computer was performing incredibly slow, and I grit my teeth upon discovering that additionally, its' computer search engine had been changed without my knowledge. I tried to understand why and when the change occurred while attempting to "clean" it with minimal and unenthusiastic tech knowledge. Meanwhile, I changed work hats every time a customer walked through the door.

131

OFF with the frustrating computer work hat and ON with the "Can I help you? I've all the time in the world for you" hat. During my alternating job duties, the store phone kept ringing. The caller ID cited an 800 number, so I ignored it.

I called my husband to help clean the computer files, and he, sensing a tantrum, showed up to assist (brave soul). He began by looking at the search history. It was during this analysis that brought to light a disturbing pattern of employee online computer searches. Add to that, casual and frequent downloads, and the integrity of my work computer were now in serious question. The history log recorded the following search during an employee shift, one of many, many searches. On this particular day, the store opened at 10:00 am, and between 11:26 and 11:28, the employee hit such keys as "return," "yes," and "accept" multiple times, accepting a change in my search engine. The actual log, in part, is as follows:

10:13 Local news channel 4

10:37 Dallas transgender woman found dead on street

10:39 Witnesses sought in suspicious death of man at local Casino

10:42 Arnold Schwarzenegger got kicked in the back while he was in South Africa

10:58 Breaking news, weather, radar, sports and traffic

11:21 Bios/news channel 4

132

11:25 Local news channel 2

11:26 Breaking news by headlines

11:26 Search engine web store

11:26 Patch – local news breaking, events, discussions

11:26 Breaking news by headlines

11:26 Breaking news chrome web store

11:27 Uninstall Survey

11:27 Latest news, newsbreak

11:28 online news

11:28 search engine change

11:29 local news

We found the problem, but it brought into question, "How much 'stuff' is searched on this computer?" I hesitantly searched the logs from other days to find endless searches, shopping, and downloads. Ignorance is bliss, and this new knowledge made me cringe. The more I saw, the more my feelers went down. Finally, I was forced to institute a no recess time on the computer.

But the day didn't end there, not by a longshot. During this disturbing discovery of computer issues, the phone continued to ring from the unidentified 800 number. I was a pressure cooker. Only to cease the ringing, I answered the phone while frothing at the mouth…

Me: Hello?

Him: (insert heavy accent) This is iCloud support; we are calling to tell you your account has been compromised.

Me: What account?

Him: Your iCloud account.

Me: What are you talking about?

Him: Your account has been compromised, and you are in great danger!

Me: What danger, what kind of danger, what are you talking about?

Him: Your iCloud account has been seriously compromised, and your identity can be used to rob banks or worse! (yes, he seriously said to rob banks or worse)

Me: What account, you tell me what account, you have all the information, tell me exactly what account, my phone? My computer? What? I can't understand what you're talking about?!

He caught me off-guard when he broke in with, "Would you let me talk! I'm saying your account has been compromised," to which I broke in yet again with ever-increasing frustration and volume, and he hung up on me! After some research of my own, I was able to link the caller ID number and name to a phishing scam to get my personal information. The caller hadn't counted on the likes of me as I unintentionally spun the table and got

134

him to hang up. No doubt he had some choice names for me. I was a bad girl, and about to get worse.

A customer walked in for the grand finale while I thought to myself, "Oh no!" I knew her well from previous visits and anticipated a challenge to my already fragile temper. She consistently had a tough time with decisions; it looked like there'd be a collision with my bad day. She started just as she had the other visits:

Her: Do you have anything for really dry skin?

Me: Yes, we do; we have a new product specifically for hydrating dry skin.

Her: Does it have SPF?

Me: Well, no, this one doesn't, but it'll take care of your dry skin!

Her: I want SPF. Would the day cream with SPF take care of my dry skin?

Me: Well, there's certainly some hydrating qualities about the day cream with SPF.

Her: But I want something specifically for dry skin; I have really dry skin.

Me: Well, you might want to get both products, use the day cream, and get your SPF, then use the product specifically for really dry skin, like yours, at night.

Her: Well, can't I use just the day cream?

Me: You could, like I mentioned, it does have hydrating qualities; it just won't be AS hydrating as the product specifically for hydrating.

Her: Then I'll get the one specifically for hydrating, but I wanted the SPF.

She caught me off guard; I was exhausted. Predictably she returned the product several days later. Although I can't always provide a mega product, I certainly could have provided a better explanation and offered more options. I seriously failed in making her feel good about her purchase. Lesson learned: take the proper time and effort to make the customer feel good about their purchase, even when you ARE having a bad day.

Not all days layered problems to that extent. More often than not, it fell along the lines of multitasking patience with listening... like the phone call from Rose. She called the store during a reasonably busy spell, and I could tell just 30 seconds into it that it wouldn't be a short phone call. After an overly long description of a discontinued product that Rose loved, I delivered the bad news:

Me: I'm so sorry, but that product is discontinued.

Rose: It can't be, I'm online, and I see it.

Me: You might be on eBay; that website often has discontinued items.

Rose: eBay? What's eBay? I'm looking at it; it's right here; they must still make it.

Me: No, it's discontinued. It's just that any Joe Blow can sell discontinued things online.

Rose: Joe Who?

Me: No, that's just an expression.

Rose: It makes my skin so smooth, and you should see what it does for my pores!

Me: I'm sure it does, and it's unfortunate, but I can't get it anymore. We have similar products; maybe...

The futile back and forth lasted 15 minutes. Rose would say, "I love it," and I said, "I can't get it" while trying to explain that her favorite product was gone, it's probably never coming back, but there are options. Rose didn't want options. I rang up customers throughout the phone call, and they smiled as they caught snippets of my unsuccessful attempts to appease Rose. Joe Who?

My expectations didn't include a layering of problems. I underestimated challenges, and overestimated my energy.

In reality, a small business is frequently worked solo and involves an unpredictable lineup of problems. If you're lucky, they come at you one at a time. If you're not, well, two words: wine and chocolate.

"Oh No! Here we go again!"

Chapter 16
A Roller Coaster of Emotions

Would I do it again? My gut response is, "Absolutely not." All too clear are my prayers to get me out of it and the feeling of disbelief that I put myself in that position in the first place. The overwhelming dread that washed over me as bills mushroomed into the perfect storm once again is still all too fresh in my mind. The perfect storm is the words my husband used as he grumbled while paying the usual and steady bills that collided with quarterly, and even worse, unexpected bills. Those situations had two options: throw in the towel and cut your losses or whip out the second mortgage checkbook to save the day yet again. I laid awake many nights and would tell myself, "Just go to sleep; there's nothing you can do about it now." It's not a good feeling.

Conversely, in writing this book, I laughed a lot. It was refreshing to know impossible odds were overcome. I grew from an introvert into a more confident person. I was never comfortable in social situations, but I learned that people soften their tone quickly if I soften mine first. It was something I never even attempted in the past and was now forced upon me out of necessity. That was a good thing.

> "Because if you take a risk, you just might find what you're looking for."
> – Susane Colasanti, author

I'm a big believer in the expression that everything is meant to be. The upshot, I essentially earned a college degree in business the hard way. It cost just about the same! Phrases like inventory assets and end-of-year losses became a part of my vocabulary. In addition to my applied degree in business, I obtained an unexpected one in psychology. If I'd seen a realistic vision of the trials ahead of me, I might have never opened my own business. That would be a shame in many respects as I like the person I've become from this experience.

I experienced the advantages of being a small store, making that little difference for a small group of people. My opportunity to walk elderly customers to their cars, or rush to the front door to open it for them, was undeniably appreciated. I was able to take the time to interpret for those who were either deaf or spoke little to no English, prompting me to begin to learn a second language. A small group of people with severe disabilities found comfort in a low-key, small store setting. I am grateful to have been able to provide it.

Owning a store primarily for women gave me a unique perspective into the roller coaster of expectations for women in each decade of their life. The unrealistic pressures for women to look and stay young are clear and unfortunate. Supermodel Paulina Porizkova said, "It's really freaking hard to be a woman. And it's really freaking hard to be a woman over 50 because we really get dismissed from the table. We have, like, a weird period between, you're J-Lo looking fabulous and then Betty White. And there's kind of like a dead zone between the two." She's right, and I saw it every day.

What caught me off guard were the young girls brought in by mothers, grandmothers, and aunts to buy their first set of makeup. I get it, better they buy their first makeup with some supervision, but it was frustrating to see they felt pressure from society at that very young age. Some of them were as young as ten years old. Each time I looked at their flawless skin and naturally long eyelashes and thought what a shame it was to alter that. I tried to gear them towards minimal makeup like a tinted moisturizer instead of foundation or lip balm instead of the heavier lip glosses and stains. I cringed when they wanted eye shadow or eyeliner.

Although the stories within represent a smaller fraction of people, they are the ones that got my attention. The fact is that the bulk of my customers put a smile on my face. Over the years, I learned much truth about Pareto's Principle, the 80/20 rule. Eighty percent of a company's revenue is generated by 20 percent of the customers. Eighty percent of complaints come from 20 percent of the customers, and it took me a long time to not take it as a personal attack. This is one of the latter:

A customer marches in with a look of irritation and asks for rouge with a curt tone. Tending to her needs, we walk over to the rouge/blush section. Pointing out both the crème blushes and the pressed powder blushes, I mentioned the latter as the better seller. Forgetting the curt tone and initial march for a moment, I comfortably asked, "Do you want a pressed powder?" Her voice escalates as she slowly says, ROOOOOUGE," as if that line had already been crossed. My response was polite enough as I tried to minimize my raising hackles, "Yes, but would you like it in a pressed powder," and she repeated, "I want ROOOOOUGE, the stuff that goes on your face, it's in a square box, and it's not like those, it's all filled in," once again, speaking to me like I'm an imbecile. Hackles, fully raised now, I begin to say, "I think the one you had might be discon," to which she heatedly breaks in, "Yes, I know, DISCONTINUED, every time I find something decent, they discontinue it!" At this point, her overreaction is almost humorous. Yet I calmly continue by asking, "Do you have your old package?" She says, "Yes, I have it, but I'm not going to get it; I'm NOT coming back, I'm going to Walgreens!"

Years before this incident, her actions could have made me cry. Now I was several years into the business and was able to grin and say to myself, "WOW!" and even get a small chuckle from it. I can only assume she was having a bad day, and I took the brunt of it, but, wow!

The tears the laughs the lessons learned
The products bought and then returned
The skin that was thin
Is now like buckskin
A degree in resilience well-earned

More common are the customers who come in with vague descriptions that help, but not much. For example, they'll say, "I'd like the liquid foundation but can't remember what color I use, but I know beige is in the name." I wanted to help as they were so happy in that they could remember at least part of the proper name. Regrettably, the word beige is in Pink Beige, Light Beige, Medium Beige, Dark Beige, Natural Beige, Cream Beige, Honey Beige, Pure Beige, Sand Beige, and Warm Beige. Or they'll say it was in a black container (they're all in a black container). Or worse yet, it was in a blue container, to which I truthfully say, "Our products haven't been in a blue container for a couple of decades." But, of course, this comment draws the inevitable denial of how old that product they're still using indeed is by their quick and predictable response, "I just bought it six months ago." Uh, huh. One step worse than vague is no basis of description, leaving me to ponder the mystic art of mind reading and the fact that I have not entirely mastered it…

There are some weird moments in working with the public that have you questioning your sanity. For example, I was approached by a female customer who stated, "I want a can of stuff. You gave me some behind the counter the last time I was here." This dialog sounded a lot like a drug deal had gone down at some point. As I waited for the rest of the sentence, my blank face prompted her to repeat herself. She repeated, "You gave me some the last time I was here," her hands now outstretched with that, "What's wrong with you?" look on her face. She was obviously angered and flustered at my

143

lack of mindreading skills and unsympathetic that many faces and transactions pass my way (plus I have a memory like a jellyfish). I, too, was becoming flustered as this was quickly becoming a touchy subject. The baffling questioning continued something like this:

Me: What was it for?

Her: I can't remember.

Me: Did you keep the package?

Her: No.

Me: Do you remember if it was a jar or in a tube?

Her: No.

She tossed me the stink eye and the "Boy, are you stupid" look before leaving with disgust. Reluctantly I surrender, in that perhaps, women do have higher expectations for people to read their minds. Ouch!

Though problematic customers make fun stories, there were plenty of kind (bordering on warm and fuzzy) people in the 80 percent.

"If you're looking at things with the right set of eyes, people are endlessly fascinating. And then, of course, if you look at it the wrong way, then the whole world is horrible and tedious and boring. That's the battle, really, to keep looking at the world in the right way."
– John Cusak

For example, one of my regular customers handcrafted a Christmas tree ornament from year to year for my disabled son. Every year she would ask about his current likes, then reappear, holding a thoughtful and wrapped package for him. One day, I felt sorry for myself and mumbled like a big baby, "Nobody goes out of their way for me," then quickly stopped when I remembered her. Yes, some go above and beyond, really do care, and make a huge, huge difference. The kindness she extended will touch me for a lifetime.

As far as emotions go, the most powerful ball of wax has to revolve around each Christmas season. Besides the all too obvious reason: sales literally went up over 50% in December, there was simply a magic surrounding it all. With the increased foot traffic, it felt like the bustling little store that I had always envisioned. Additionally, being decorated for Christmas, it "felt" like something out of a Hallmark Christmas movie. Though I drove my employees crazy by playing the movie *It's a Wonderful Life* over and over, the shoppers would quite literally stop in their tracks, and say things like, "oh, I LOVE this movie!" Sometimes they would take a seat and watch the movie for a while. It felt good to add a little dose of feel-good to the outside world that was moving way too fast. I had several customers come in and remark, with voices still shaking, about the road rage taking place in the parking lot and beyond. They were able to take in down a notch in this much slower paced environment.

I'll add with all honesty, most of my customers were sweet, polite, considerate people. I've been changed by those who went out of their way for me, lit up my day by the smile they had upon greeting me or had the patience and understanding to forgive me when I was clearly wrong. I've had a few who stopped and prayed with me and for me. They prayed for my friends and family, right there at the register after hearing my concerns. They sometimes took me out of my comfort zone but helped me grow by doing so.

Watching the years tick by, contemplating the "circle of life" from a unique perspective within my little pool of customers was bittersweet. My coworkers and I were privy to quite a bit of intimate customer information and heartbreaking stories. I had a sweet customer who was battling cancer for years, one of many, unfortunately. She was an attractive woman inside and out, classy, and very upbeat. She came in regularly, probably every month or two, so I knew she was doing ok for quite some time. She appeared to be doing well; then it seemed she got very sick, very fast. And then she disappeared. I know some customers by name, but most were familiar only by their face and their story. I realized she had likely passed away, but it was sobering as I looked for her and wondered. She often spoke of her strong faith and how she wasn't afraid, regardless of the outcome. She had an enviable, positive attitude, and it was moving.

During my first year, a friendly mother and daughter came in together and often. I enjoyed their company and watched for nearly a decade as the daughter got married, and had her first baby, then her second baby, and finally a third. It put time, and its' shockingly fast pace, in perspective.

My expectations were pretty conventional regarding opening, operating, and ultimately closing my small store. I certainly didn't expect much emotion, not did I expect that the faces, voices and stories would stay with me a lifetime, but they will.

In reality, I ran the scale of emotions. Every significant interaction changed me. Though you can say that about most anything in life, these moments combined were, for me, truly "life-changing." My lifetime of annoyingly repetitive prayers was for exactly what I was to receive by operating that little store. I had an about-face with confidence, and although my patience will probably never be perfect, it went from a two to maybe a seven?

"I've come from being afraid of everything to being fearful of very little"

Chapter 17
Lessons Learned

The common belief that it takes three to five years until a business turns a profit turned into something much longer. The realization struck that although it's turning a profit, it's not much of one. Earnings can be wiped out quickly by a leaky roof or a broken HVAC. The point-of-sale system could need an upgrade, or the snow removal for the year could deliver a hefty blow to the pocketbook. You can't control the weather. The same weather conditions you pay to have salted and snowplowed also took away considerable business while it was happening; it doesn't seem fair that it would deliver a second punch.

If it's raining or snowing, shoppers won't come. If it's icy, they certainly won't, and if they're merely predicting it, they won't come either. If it's too hot or vice versa, goodbye customer. Finally, if it's perfect and hasn't been for a while, they won't come because they want to enjoy the beautiful weather. Get the picture?

I sat in the dentists' chair during one such weather fiasco when he asked how things were going. I answered with honesty, "not so good," and went on a roll about how the rough winter pulled my January numbers down 23 percent! Surprisingly he chimed in with, "here too!" He added that if they so much call for inclement weather, people will preemptively cancel their appointments. Misery loves company, and validation is always welcome.

149

During a five-hour shift on a pathetically slow day, the store had only brought in $15 in total sales. The employee was paid $14/hour; do the math. The weather wasn't even bad; there was just a threat of bad weather. Thanks to fanatical weather reports, we found ourselves in negative numbers due to a simple threat. What used to be regular weather occurrences now trigger doomsday reports for higher ratings. They're peppered with enough threats to scare just about everyone into staying home. It kills any chance of regular traffic flow, even if the weather never turns. In general, people are held hostage by worst-case scenarios, even if they live a mere 15 minutes away.

There are days when I know without a doubt, the amount of money earned won't cover payroll. Yet that nagging voice to be responsibly open haunts me into it. Profit or not, my landlord will still get his rent, I will pay my employees, and the utility companies will get their bills paid. The only thing that keeps a business going is the hopeful thought of, "Maybe, just maybe, things will take a major turn for the better."

I wouldn't go so far as to call myself irresponsible, but I could've put my nose to the grindstone more in paying off the initial business loan. Several years into store ownership, we squeaked in family vacations; that money would've gone a long way towards the loan. However, if I had to choose again, I'd still choose the vacations. You never know what tomorrow will bring, and owning a small business is tough on the entire family. We needed a break, even if only for a bit.

There were carrots along the way. I was able to win some fantastic trips from my parent company for my husband and myself, including whale watching in Hawaii (following picture), horseback riding near Vegas (also pictured), Hollywood, Disney World, and Punta Cana.

We probably wouldn't have done any of it had they not been part of the entire package. But, still emphasizing that a traditional job with a regular paycheck would have been safer with less stress, there were perks. The trips, some good memories, and most of all, the personal growth made it worth the while. At least that's what I tell myself.

Lastly, what would I have done differently? I wouldn't have asked store owners how to do something. Instead, I would have asked them, "What had you in tears?"

Yes, there was a business plan, but it was just a start, and it was created more to satisfy the company's checklist from whom I purchased my product and less for myself. They even told me, "That's one of the best business plans we've ever seen," but in hindsight, I'm thinking to myself, "Well, it didn't do a thing for me."

Having that loan hanging over your head is a menacing thing. Anything that messed with that goal should have been questioned. I don't propose taking all the enjoyment out of life, but simply put, I wasn't strict enough; this isn't a game.

Perhaps I could've avoided some pitfalls if my actions were more like the all business/no-nonsense Harriet Oleson (the shopkeeper character from the TV series Little House on the Prairie). The money spent, the things given away, was a bit irresponsible. I don't regret everything, but I should have been more careful.

It was a bad habit to give discounts to numerous customers, varying from 25 percent to a whopping 40-50 percent. I couldn't remember to whom I gave them or how much, so I would carelessly give them one. With the advantage of retrospect, here are some of my lessons:

1. Be careful with the initial setup. While your retail space's overall impression is critical, there's a fine line between a good impression and going over the top with a flippant attitude.
2. Watch the number of freebies offered. From chocolate at the register to unrestrained donations, the costs can get out of hand quickly. I thought it'd be fun to have free chocolate until it felt as though that bowl was feeding customers their lunch. As I cut costs, one customer boldly complained about the variety of chocolate as if beggars could indeed be choosers.
3. Be careful with bank fees; interview several banks to get a gut feeling of who will treat you like an old friend. I sometimes felt I was treated with the same detached once-over you get at the airport security line. No thank you.

4. When it comes to marking down products on the slightest hint of a request, don't.

5. Keep a tight rein on pay and raises; you can't easily backtrack without looking like a putz. Pay enough to keep honest employees, but don't throw money away; it just isn't there in the early years. Also, delegate work to those already being paid. In flying solo, I cheated myself and even my employees, for that matter. Social media and the Chamber of Commerce's perks are both things that I neither had the time or the energy to do. Designating more tasks to employees sitting idle in their spare time could have made the difference between struggling and cruising along.

6. Take the time for meticulous bookkeeping records to write off expenses effectively. I shudder to think what may have been lost in this area with shrinkage and legitimate write-offs.

7. Don't make rash assumptions when choosing your retail space. My decision was hasty with a "seems ok" approach. Consider if you can afford a space in a fully occupied area, preferably with food nearby; restaurants are stable, and people like to eat. After several years in my location, I considered moving to a busier section of the plaza. But, it was another risk I was unwilling to take nor had the energy to undertake.

8. Institute a store credit mentality when handing out refunds without a receipt or after a certain amount of time. I was too quick to hand back cash when a credit would have sufficed. Enforcing rules is easily validated when mirroring the well-known chain stores, use their well-researched and established guidelines.

9. The point-of-sale system is a big purchase, and the one I bought was overkill for the store's size. Consider preowned and try to eliminate the yearly support contract by having two less expensive systems, so you have a backup. Weigh your options; there's a lot of people that want your business on this one.

At the end of my adventure, I have a confidence I never thought I would have, along with incredible memories. I'll remember the customers who called me by name and treated me like a friend. I'll remember the interesting characters, like the customer who carried her phone throughout the store, left on speaker, while her friend wailed and blubbered on the other end. She not only casually shopped but seemed oblivious to my presence a mere five or ten feet away bearing witness to it all.

I'll also smile when thinking of the elderly gentleman that strolled in and just knew I could help him when he stated, "I need a battery for my flip phone." He followed up with a quick demonstration and added, "See, I push the button, and nothing happens." I weaved him through the displays of lipsticks, lotions, perfumes, and not a cell phone or battery in sight, to my computer, where a quick google search was performed. I found and directed him to the nearest store that could indeed replace the battery on his flip phone. It felt good to be in a position to help.

What IS a successful store? If you're looking for one you can hire out, sit back, and collect the profit, you might be sorely disappointed. On the other hand, some people do it and even own multiple franchises. If you're looking for one that you pour your heart and soul into, enjoying the benefits by doing what you love, that's possible also. Either way, there's a risk, and you have to answer the question, "Can I afford to lose everything put into this?"

I've come from being afraid of everything to being fearful of very little. The unique opportunity to learn from a wide variety of people was a gift. It's not that I think so much of myself now; it's that I don't think so little.

I've been asked that question a lot. Would I do it again? Owning your own business can be gratifying. It allows for freedom and offers personal growth. On the other hand, I wouldn't recommend doing it if you have too much on your plate, and honestly, that describes most people nowadays. My plate was full, emotionally and physically. It was too much to think I could handle opening and operating a store primarily by myself with a family at home. Yes, I'm glad I did it because I grew as a person, but it was somewhat at the expense of myself and my family life, so that in itself is a conflicting statement.

156

My answer would lie more along the lines of going for it, IF you have a relatively cleared plate. It would help if you also had support, which is why so many small businesses were traditionally family-owned; it makes a lot of sense. My initial decision-making revolved around how so many women tend to think, we believe that we can do it all, and we can't. There were times I was truly overwhelmed.

My expectations were so fundamental in envisioning an old-fashioned general store. I imagined not a whole lot of customers but enough to turn a good profit. I had a straightforward but naïve mentality of product sales minus product costs equal gain.

In reality, I had a lot to learn, and at times was in over my head. Things have changed too much for the small business. But the advantages remain for both the owner and the customers. A friendly and personal setting offers a welcoming environment for the customer, with flexibility and a sense of pride for the store owners. The corner stores, the *Cheers* type taverns, and the *Monk's Café* type diners are unmatched. We would lose a lot if we lost our small businesses, approachable staff, and the connections created.

"Maybe, just maybe…"

Chapter 18
Retail Roulette

Running a small retail business is a lot like spinning a roulette wheel. You can win big, you could lose everything, or there's a decent chance that you'll do ok. The problem is, even after you've landed on a good space, you MUST take another spin at the wheel.

On a particular day in March 2020, the wheel landed on Covid-19. I sounded like a broken record during the near-decade of store ownership and routinely complained and threatened to throw in the towel. I can safely assume that more than one family member, friend, or acquaintance rolled their eyes and thought, "Just shut up and do it already." It seemed this time my mind may be made up for me.

Numbers begin to pull ahead
Could be our chance to get out of the red
But an epidemic
A crazy pandemic
Set us back once again instead

Not in a million years did I imagine running orders out to cars wearing a mask over my face and dog poop bags over my hands because real vinyl gloves were long gone. It was accompanied by my letting them know how genuinely appreciated their support was. I sincerely valued those customers who had my back and showed up for curbside deliveries but could also see that I was in hot

159

water. Words like liquidation, freak out mode, and mounting debt went through my head like wildfire.

In March of 2020, it was clear that things were going to get weird. Just a few weeks earlier, during what began as my most promising year yet, I pondered unfamiliar territory and thought to myself, "Huh, maybe it WOULD make sense to hold onto the store." That thought went out the window pretty quick. January and February were up around 15 percent from the previous year, a pretty impressive start to the year considering 2-3 percent is deemed respectable for an established business. When Covid-19 reared its' head, I began to see a dramatic turn in mid-March. Knowing that if I were to continue making my rent, significant changes would need to occur quickly. I didn't realize how fast. The spiral of events went down within only two to three weeks.

MARCH 1-7, 2020 The first week in March brought in average sales numbers.

MARCH 8-21, 2020 The second and third weeks were down by 25 percent and showed the same wild and erratic swings the stock market was showing. It took years to keep calm and accept daily sales fluctuations, but this was heart wrenching.

MARCH 16TH, 2020 I sent a text to all four of the part-time employees that read, "Numbers are dropping at the store, and if anyone can sacrifice a few hours back to me, I'd appreciate it until the end of this month, and then I'll reanalyze. I'm getting worried about the bills."

The first to reply was my part-timer that worked three part-time jobs. Unbeknownst to me, she had already been laid off from her other two jobs. She understood despite her situation, but I felt like a heel adding to her burden. The other three responded shortly afterward, and all with a sympathetic demeanor. On March 16th, I took away half of their hours, and apologized with sincerity. Adding that we'd talk about April later, none of us could imagine the depth of that conversation.

MARCH 21ST, 2020 A mere five days later, things changed dramatically as the big box stores around me closed temporarily but abruptly. Without them, I'm a goner. I sent out another text to my employees, stating, "With almost zero-foot traffic, I need to make significant changes. The bulk of the stores around me are closed. There is enough for this Friday's payroll but not even close to enough for rent. I'm changing store hours, and I'll be working all of them myself, but please understand it's not what I want. There's no telling if and when hours will go back to normal, especially if the city and county close non-essential stores. Sorry about all the changes and uncertainty."

Neither text message felt good sending, but the second and far more severe of the two was a no-brainer. It had to be done. On March 22nd, my store brought in total sales of $31. It was increasingly clear I was in new, scary territory. There was, however, a steady stream of customers filing into the liquor store two doors down from me. They were doing a rip-roaring business.

MARCH 23RD, 2020 My store was deemed non-essential and needed to close to the already diminished foot traffic. Luckily for the liquor store two doors down, they were designated essential and seemed to have a dramatic increase in sales. I stared out of my storefront window and watched as it became crystal clear what the new priorities were. People were wheeling carts of liquor out to their cars.

I had a trickle of money coming in from online sales, but panic mode set in when the stark realization of rent, utilities, and outstanding balances started bouncing around. After almost nine years in business, bills were still paid from month to month, and even worse, some were in arrears. So maybe I wasn't sitting as pretty as previously thought when coming to this bump in the road.

My first thought was to liquidate, and quick, as I wiped the sweat from my upper lip. However, it was utterly unrealistic. There would be no way to liquidate much of anything for months until this thing went away. To close, I would have to vacate and bring EVERYTHING home. We had just downsized into a small condo with no basement. Storing the product in the garage could damage it as the weather warmed; keeping it in the house would be cumbersome and overwhelming. Just as overwhelming was the looming and potentially ballooning debt with partial but ongoing bills. I found myself cornered, like a rat, and desperate animals do desperate things. I contacted my landlord for advice.

It was clear I was one of the last tenants to call; his response seemed thought out and thorough. He was understanding and considerate; after all, this was his livelihood as well. For the time being, I would be responsible for only the triple net portion of my rent, hence less than a third of my typical monthly payment. The triple net would cover his ongoing expenses, including real estate taxes, insurance, and maintenance. The bottom line, I still needed to come up with partial rent, utilities, and outstanding bills—the burden of owning a business set in again. It was clear all along that there would be a risk; I just felt we had largely beaten it. A pandemic? I didn't see THAT coming.

In the meantime, my store joined the ranks of those small businesses trying to improvise. My efforts focused on selling what could be sold with curbside deliveries; it was cumbersome. Customers would inevitably show up simultaneously, and the wholly organized person I once was became very agitated and unorganized with this new routine. The only thing I knew about cross-contamination was learned from the T.V. show M*A*S*H. My gut feeling was that I wouldn't pass any inspections with my improvised roll of dog poop bags.

My mood further sunk as my steamy breath leeched out of my mask, fogging my glasses and raising my blood pressure. And notes to self, "Apologize to the dentist, brush teeth more, gargle with like, Listerine." Another customer remarked that the material her mask was made from "smelled like a zoo." I kept my reply to myself, "Speaking from experience, I don't think it's the mask."

When the customers showed up in tandem, I began clumsily working on one order with my bag-covered hands while ignoring the second phone call coming in. Of course, it's not my nature to ignore any phone call. My husband was looking on as my panic mode turned into a comical Lucille Ball episode, and he quipped, "Someday you'll look back and this and laaaaaaugh." Laugh?

What I did laugh at was an experience with an older customer that called in an order. She instructed me to deliver it to her car through the passenger side window as her drivers' side window was inoperable. I began to reach through the opening when a very serious growl greeted me from her small but protective dog. As if trained to perform in the movies, he bared his teeth while his lips quivered around them. For a dog his size (about three pounds), he looked menacing. I've learned from countless hours volunteering at humane societies, "Be wary of big dogs, be very wary of small dogs." Like every other dog owner on the planet, she cackled and said, "Oh, don't worry, he doesn't bite." I made attempt number two and backed off once again to the grrrrr. My customers' giggling convinced me to try again, so after judging an approximate snapping zone, I snaked my arm as far from this feisty animal as humanly possible. She was still laughing when she pulled away; I'm so glad I was fodder for her amusement.

My front door remained locked during curbside deliveries, except the day it was propped open for a shipment. A lady wandered in like a stray cat but was quickly shooed away like a rodent; I only lacked the broom to push her. I felt terrible as she looked a bit pathetic and said, "I just want to go somewhere so bad." This bizarre new norm was all so weird.

On the more positive side was the genuine care my loyal customers sent my way as they supported me with curbside pickups, online orders, and kind words. Their sincere concern over the years has changed me from a cynic to a much more content person. What I once believed to be an unusual thing were, in fact, numerous and humbling experiences. How rare it is, or so I thought, to have an acquaintance make eye contact and genuinely say, "Are you doing ok?" or "Hang in there." Yet, I experienced it many times, especially during this event. It drove home the powerful impact of words.

Two months after closing temporarily, I reopened with the other non-essential businesses. There were new rules and a new mindset as I shortened my hours and proceeded slightly on edge. Armed with a mask, anti-bacterial gel, anti-bacterial wipes, a spray bottle with bleach/water, and a freakish amount of handwashing, my new and surreal routine started back along with everyone else. The front door was propped open to make it evident that the store was indeed open for business. It was almost cute as people tiptoed in a few steps and craned their necks, asking, "Is it ok if I come in?"

One customer sneezed at the register and immediately looked up at me with widened, apologetic eyes as if she had just committed a capital crime. She said, "I promise! It's just allergies!" It wasn't long before I had my first lonely customer. It was only day one. She lingered at the cash register, without a mask, while another masked customer patiently waited her turn six feet away. She was in no hurry and began telling me about her relatives, their likes, and dislikes, including what kind of cookies they liked. She interjected several coughs during her chatter, followed by a slightly snarky, "Oh, don't worry, I ain't got that thing." Really? The only reassuring notion was her deep, raspy but likely her natural voice, so there was little doubt that she did indeed cough often. But still.

If you know me, you know I loathe political correctness. Yet, I posted a politically correct sign near the register to make everyone comfortable in those early first few days and weeks. It read, "We miss our customers, but to follow guidelines, please make your visit as brief as possible for everyone's safety; thanks!" One older gentleman went right back into old habits by thoroughly scanning my counter after his purchase and asking, "You don't have any candy?" The candy jar had been removed years before, so it'd been a while since he'd been in the store, and the virus clearly wasn't his number one concern; it made me smile. Another lady told me that she had to "stray" and purchase makeup at the grocery store while my store was closed, but she hated it so much that she threw it away. That was music to my ears.

166

On day four of reopening, I had a minor meltdown that only another woman could understand. The stress of lingering store bills coupled with an uncertain future for the store led me to drink more wine the evening before than I rightly should have. I was nursing my wounds with a big wedge of Oreo cookie pie because, as we all know, a hangover can only be cured by eating more crap. A female customer took note of my lunch choice by saying, "That looks like a good lunch." It was her look more than her comment that spoke volumes and that she understood my mood. I smiled and replied, "Yeah, it's one of those days." Now a guy would look at that pie and give me the one raised eyebrow look that made me feel worse than I already did. But, my female counterpart was more like, "I feel your pain, sister."

Indeed, there were no expectations regarding a pandemic or nationwide shutdown. I anticipated only everyday things because, in my lifetime, I'd never experienced anything out of the norm for any length of time.

In reality, I learned nothing is off-limits, and this new awakening was unsettling. However, it was humbling to witness the amount of support my customers showed as they united around me like an extended family.

"Closing the store is the right thing to do, just keep telling yourself that"

Chapter 19
Maybe Not

The store so narrowly made it for years, nine years. My reluctant conclusion was that it had run its course during the several months of being reopened. After things began opening, there were a few weeks of robust sales, the kind that made me wonder if closing the store was the right thing to consider. Again, the phrase "maybe, just maybe" went through my head. I pulled myself back to reality, reminding myself of how many times I said maybe and how many times it ended up being "maybe not."

The chain of events from the Covid virus would undoubtedly change the brick-and-mortar stores for a long time. Those who wouldn't regularly shop online began shopping online, partly out of necessity and partly out of boredom. I loathe online shopping, but my habits changed. I had to wonder how many others changed theirs and how many would return to their old ways. There would surely be a snowball effect as people emerged from the shelter of their homes with a cautious paranoia, and the possibility of further shutdowns loomed.

Frankly, that was the number one motivation for my ultimate decision: the possibility of further shutdowns. Maybe I jumped the gun, maybe not, but going forward with crazy uncertainty was a depressing thought. And what were the chances of my getting the virus from a customer? Having a disabled son with a compromised immune system puts us in a vulnerable position.

I had researched the liquidation process and gone over it in my head many times over the years, but implementing it would be a bummer. My husband and I chose each fixture, color, and décor that filled the space; each feature had a personal story. He drew up plans and handcrafted the cash wrap that was always way too nice for a retail store. He designed two six-foot-tall shower-gel display trees that were as cute as they were functional. The floating shelves were also handmade, and they housed my trophies and awards, each representing another year and another fantastic trip, but would likely go into storage boxes. About half of them ended up in the thrift store box after I contacted a trophy shop to see if they could be repurposed. It was funny, sort of, when they told me "ugh, we've been swamped with requests; people are cleaning out their houses during the Covid lockdown."

I always thought we could sell the store and watch it live on in another hopeful and slightly disillusioned owner. The truth is, my heart and soul went into that little store, almost as if it were a living, breathing thing. If there was a stain on the carpet, I was on my hands and knees, scrubbing it out. If there were products on the shelf, slightly out of skew as I walked by, my inner voice said, "Whoa Nellie," as I backed up to straighten them. I didn't think I'd be disassembling it and watching the spiders run, as it was brought back to a depressing, stark four walls.

I will miss the statue of David that we purchased for fun décor and for whom boxer shorts were sewn to ensure no mother shopping my store would have to address her child's question of "What's that?"

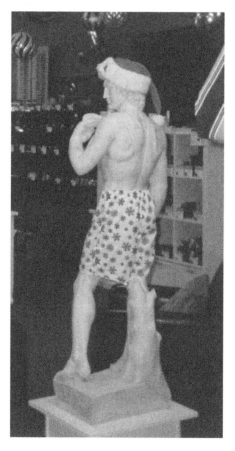

Shoot, I'll even miss seeing the makeup that those cute little rugrats jabbed their fingers into while unattended; those little stinkers! Ok, I lied, that I WON'T miss…

As I began to scan the store for the first few items to go, waves of sadness and genuine tears washed over me. It caught me off guard; I almost would rather have had a more detached response. But it was impossible to be detached from something I was so intimately acquainted with for a considerable part of my life.

Like having a child graduate from high school, you're never quite ready for another stage of your life to be over. So when the word slowly began to get out to my regular customers, I was greeted by, "OH NO!" and sad faces, choking me up repeatedly. I dug my toes in, telling myself, "Don't cry, don't cry," but it was this sadness that let me know there was something extraordinary around me.

To keep my ego in check, the hagglers made their encore appearance. Like vultures, they circled the roadkill that was still moving and made ridiculous requests on price reductions. Even though there was but one month to go, I resisted saying, "Are you nuts?" I'm so proud of myself.

In the movie "You've Got Mail," Meg Ryan plays Kathleen Kelly, a small bookstore owner. Kathleen decides to close her store after sales drop due to competition from the newly opened big-box bookstore nearby. Her friend, Birdie Conrad, played by Jean Stapleton, offers some words of comfort. She said, "Closing the store is the brave thing to do. You are daring to imagine that you could have a different life."

Once I began to accept that moving on to a different life isn't necessarily bad, the once depressing notion of closing the store started to become a feeling of a burden lifted. Working my way through yet more frustrating paperwork in preparation for closing was a helpful reminder that there would be things that I wouldn't miss. I commented to the gal that does my payroll, "I'll be glad when my business is all boxed away in a Tupper tote." She responded, "Aw, that sounds sad," to which I thought, "Yes, a little."

Like Meg Ryan's character said, "Soon it will just be a memory," but really, it's a lot of memories, and as time marches on, the good memories will surpass any bad. While it will be sad, I will no longer be accountable for submitting anything weekly, monthly, or yearly. My vacations could soon be scheduled without wondering about having my hours or duties covered. And finally, there would be no worries about a phone call that begins with, "you're not going to like this but." I wasn't a whole lot different than a farmer, with ongoing responsibilities that can't easily be put on hold for an extended time. But yes, it will be a little sad.

During my final weeks, one of my regulars came in. She had no idea about the closing when my fellow employee gave her the news. I was in the backroom when my coworker peeked around the corner and said, "There's someone who wants to talk to you." I came out, and my customer solemnly approached me while saying slowly and very sincerely, "I am so, so sorry." She said it with genuine sincerity, much like one would to console a friend after a death in the family. She let me know how the store relaxed her, that her husband knew how much the store meant to her, and that she might go home and cry, literally.

Her sincerity and words were heartwarming, and more than that, eye-opening. For years, my view of the world, especially of people, was that of a glass half empty. I let a few sour grapes get to me when, in fact, good people surrounded me, and they were validating and kind. I am blessed to walk away from my experience knowing that.

As a fun footnote, one of my last customers made for a fitting finale during the month before liquidation. She was an older lady, perhaps in her early nineties. She walked in with her cane and assertively asked for her favorite face cream. The jar she held was incredibly old, old enough to widen my eyes and raise my eyebrows one more time. Yet, in spite of her age, I knew from experience to tread lightly. It was a familiar scene, fittingly so, that went down like this:

Her: I'm looking for X product.

Me: Oh my, that one's been gone a while. (One last time, I resisted the urge to honestly say how long it's been to avoid any backlash, though she could obviously hold her own.)

Her: Why do they always discontinue the products I like?! What am I supposed to use now?

Me: People use Y product, (she stops me and breaks in)

Her: I hate that stuff.

Me: Well, Z product is pretty good; you might like that.

She settles on the Z product, and I proceed to ring up her purchase. She then makes a couple of confessions…

Her: My son doesn't know I'm out.

Me: Oh, yeah? (wondering what that means exactly)

Her: I'm pretty shaky behind the wheel.

Me: Uh oh (thinking to myself that maybe son should take away a particular set of car keys)

Contemplating closing the store throughout the years NEVER had any emotional feelings attached to it because it wasn't real yet. The feelings didn't exist for something I never believed would happen; I always thought I would pass the torch.

The reality was that many feelings, primarily of loss, would soon infiltrate my subconscious. Unsettling dreams of a dimly lit store with half-empty shelves would haunt me for a year after I locked the door for the final time. What would Freud say?

"There is something of yourself that you leave at every meeting with another person." – Mr. Rogers

Chapter 20
Goodbye Mr. Rogers Neighborhood

With three weeks to go, I began the process that made it all real —20 percent off, then 30, 40, 60, and finally, 80. I locked the door, to the public, for the final time while my one remaining employee stood by my side. She had purposely stayed late that day in case I were to fall apart completely; I appreciated the thought. I was, however, a bit embarrassed as I tried to suppress a case of the ugly cries. I could feel it coming on as my face began to contort. It took a turn for the worst when I tried to shorten its lifespan. You can't control an ugly cry; it has a life of its own. Oddly enough, merriam-webster.com actually has a definition for it, which, in part, goes like this:

> "Oprah first used the phrase in 2000, and then again in 2001, 2002, 2003, and so on. She became the daytime queen of the ugly cry, giving in to them during interviews (most notably with Mary Tyler Moore) and talking at length about them. Soon, the ugly cry was the province of women" – merriam-webster.com

So yes, though somewhat restrained, I did a short but terrifying ugly cry. I suppose the cameras caught that too. I should've just lost it; I would have felt and looked better.

I was left with a manageable box of leftover products and a three-page move-out checklist to begin to tackle. First things first, EVERYTHING from fixtures to paperwork to keepsakes had to be removed from the space.

Most of us have moved from one home to another at least once in our lifetime. It's bad enough to box up things, knowing that it all has a place to go. However, when there is no next place, and almost everything must be sold, donated, or trashed, it's a whole different ballgame. Most everything had value to someone, somewhere, but I was now paying monthly rent with no monthly income; the task at hand needed to be taken care of quickly with almost hasty decisions. Fortunately, organizing and purging things was one of my gifts. Unfortunately, the exact reason for closing my doors was keeping others from opening theirs. With the effects of the virus still lingering, there were very few new businesses looking for preowned equipment.

I was lucky in finding homes for my glass displays, all 400 squares of it—the smaller things sold during the liquidation frenzy. Unfortunately, I wasn't so fortunate with eight sheets of cherry slat wall, 64 shelves, and 192 brackets. That shelving cost $1500 initially and now lay in the donation pile alongside my pricey cash register system, another item that wasn't in high demand during a stampede of closing businesses. But with my misfortune came the opposite for several not-for-profit agencies that were happy to acquire gently used stuff for free.

My husbands' handyman skills once again attracted the eye of Sauron for one last hoorah. For those of you who don't get the Lord of the Rings reference, Sauron's eye isn't something you want pointing at you.

He dragged around his step ladder and extension ladder replacing fluorescent lights and ceiling tiles. Hundreds of holes in the walls from the shelving and artwork needed patching. He removed the sound system and wiring and repainted EVERYTHING with our oldest son's help, including the store façade, where my relatively large, lighted sign once hung.

What a depressing day that was. I stood inside my empty store, watching my now unlighted sign, lowered to the ground by crane. Then, two guys lifted this sign that was once full of life onto a flatbed truck headed for the disassembly line, or worse yet, the landfill. I didn't want to know; I instead held onto the wishful thought that someone would repurpose it.

My feelings for this sign probably sound overly dramatic. It's difficult to explain how it's possible to feel so sorry for an inanimate object, but it's how I felt. It was such a big deal to see it put up initially and definitely symbolized the start of it all. So, I guess it symbolized the end of it all to see it come down. Ugh. C'est la vie. Then I did what I do best; I rid the space of everything sellable or donatable, and then cleaned and cleaned some more. When the room echoed, it was a full-circle moment.

It was time to return to the more mundane, and the transformation was abrupt. After doing a walkthrough with the landlord and handing back the store keys, I was officially, once again, leading a more routine life. Not that I was ever a fortune 500 CEO, but at times, I was treated with a wee bit more respect than I was used to.

This new feeling became glaringly apparent when I returned my business phone equipment to the return center. What a horrible place that is; it's even worse than the DMV, if that's possible. Unlike the phone store that sells equipment and treats you somewhat human because, and only because, you might be worth a commission, the return center can be compared to an intake room in prison. It lacks only the cavity search. During intake in prison, there are rules that you damn well better follow, and I tried to follow them but still fell short. As I approached the phone company rep behind the thick acrylic window complete with a pass-through slot, I was instructed very loudly and very clearly. "Ma'am, remove all the cables and give me JUST the phone router and JUST the phone modem, then put the cables in the grey plastic bin to your left." While I'm sure she has to repeat these exact instructions throughout the day, I didn't appreciate the tone.

Thinking I was doing them a great favor, my cables were bundled together in a paper bag, assuming that like cables should be kept with like cables. The prison guard, glaring in my direction, yelled out once again as if talking to a complete imbecile, "NOT the bag, that AIN'T a trashcan!" Those keys I handed back earlier in the day almost seemed to contain some kind of magic, which I now lacked. It appeared that suddenly, I was unworthy of even marginal courtesy. Nonetheless, I could take comfort in the fact that this was familiar territory.

Thus, the store itself is gone, but I keep the memories. One last memorable, but tenderhearted customer, gave me one such memory at the tail end, during the final month. It was a return that she had, well, several returns of the same item, sort of.

She was exchanging a stuffed toy, a cute little fox named Finley. He was one of about 15 IDENTICAL stuffed toy foxes that remained in the store during liquidation. She had bought one days before and brought him back to see if one of the other ones had a cuter face. So, she put him on the counter, kind of like some poor critter being surrendered at the humane society, and selected another two off of the shelf to set beside the Finley in question, one on either side. The analysis started as I stood back and observed. She asked me, in all seriousness, "do you think this one looks cuter?" as she pointed to the one on the left. The weight of this decision seemed, weighty.

I strolled over to give my opinion of the mass-produced assembly line trio. Though they looked nearly identical to me, I agreeably agreed, why not? Then she zeroed in on Finley on the right and said, "or do you think this one is cuter?" Hmmm, decisions, decisions. Caught up in the moment, I actually DID start to see differences and personalities (pick me! pick me!). Before it got out of hand, I shook it off and blurted out, "the one on the left, the one on the left is cuter!" So off she went, with "Finley on the left" in hand.

The next day she shows up with Finley on the left, tucked under her arm (which was cute in itself), and begins the process over. This time, however, Finley's fur was in question. Again, she pulled a couple off the shelf (very well could have been rejected Finley) and lined them up. She asked me for my all-important opinion again in regards to the current dilemma, "do you think his fur looks as good as the other ones?" This time, to avoid an unnecessary attachment to the Finleys, I quickly assessed and answered. Finley on the left seemed just fine to me. She squirmed a bit but then reluctantly agreed, and off she went. Finley on the left made the cut, though I have the feeling, when Finley's owner is either reading or eating breakfast, she'll stop mid-read or mid-chew, and look at Finley with that, "I'm still not quite sure about you" look. Hmmm.

Yes, I will miss the people. For years to come, if you see me with a slight smile, I just might be thinking, "My son doesn't know I'm out." If I'm biting my lip and shaking my head no, for no apparent reason, I might be cringing about the day I decided to play the movie *The Goodbye Girl,* and that scene, and the not-so-perfect timing.

I will miss the window washing guy, the UPS guy, and the neighboring store employees trekking into their workplaces every day, rounding off the "Mr. Rogers Neighborhood" feeling.

And lastly, I will miss my employees. They offered companionship, so I wasn't alone while learning and maturing in this somewhat weird experience. Anyone who knows me knows I'm not a people person. But I would be remiss if I didn't admit that it's these same people that give me a sense of routine and normality in a crazy world.

My husband wisecracked, "You're going to be solely responsible for halting any new small businesses with this frank and daunting assessment of running one." I doubt it, and I hope not. Instead, I hope that I'm responsible for an increase in support of small businesses. I hope that instead, there is greater awareness of their struggles and, more importantly, what they offer. Friendships, a low-stress atmosphere, personal attention are all irreplaceable by the big box stores. And for the icing on the cake, shoppers will be part of why the small business owner, an actual person, does a happy dance.

184

about the author

Carol McManus blends wit with experience to pass along knowledge while grabbing the readers' attention with humor. Forever searching for the meaning of life, she gained insight into what life has to offer working as a library minion, dental assistant, cashier, computer entry zombie, rotisserie chicken wrangler, substitute teacher (that was a brief one), store owner, and finally, writer. Battling a dubious self-confidence, she has risen to the occasion celebrating that small, almost nonexistent nub of a gene that never gave up screaming, "You can do it!" When she's not writing, you might find Carol rereading a James Herriot book, who can easily evoke her laughter and tears. When she wants to feel better about her own life, she'll watch Breaking Bad on Netflix again. After toggling between the states of Illinois, Virginia, Washington and Missouri, she has settled in Missouri with her husband, two sons, and dog Lucy. Occasionally they take to the road in their roving R.V./rig "Ruby Toobie." Carol shares dual citizenship with the U.S. and Canada, torn between drinking tea from a really big mug or sipping it from a bone china teacup, with pinky raised.

186

I hope you enjoyed reading my book as much as I enjoyed writing it! If you liked reading Adventures in Small Business, I would appreciate it if you shared your experience with an online review. This feedback helps me in addition to future readers. To leave a review on Amazon, simply log in, find my book, scroll down to the bottom of the page and find the reviews, then hit the button that says "Write a customer review." I appreciate your time, thank you so much! - C.L. McManus

Made in the USA
Monee, IL
01 December 2021